P9-DFK-822

Char-Broil
Grilling's Juicy Little Secret™
TRU INFRARED™
grilling
SURF AND TURF

CB's Famous Smoked Salmon, page 34

CREATIVE
HOMEOWNER®

140 SAVORY RECIPES FOR SIZZLE ON THE GRILL

CREATIVE HOMEOWNER®, Upper Saddle River, New Jersey

CREATIVE HOMEOWNER®

A Division of Federal Marketing Corp.
Upper Saddle River, NJ

Char-Broil GRILLING SURF AND TURF

SENIOR EDITOR Kathie Robitz
CONTRIBUTING EDITOR Barry "CB" Martin
PROOFREADER Sara M. Markowitz
INDEXER Erica Caridio, The Last Word
PRINCIPAL PHOTOGRAPHERS Glenn E. Teitell, Dyne Benner (food stylist), Freeze Frame Studio; Glenn Moores, Trudy Hewer (food stylist), Stuart Marston (grill chef), Contact Jupiter, Inc. (photo coordinator)
DIGITAL IMAGING SPECIALIST Mary Dolan
DESIGN AND LAYOUT David Geer

CREATIVE HOMEOWNER

VICE PRESIDENT AND PUBLISHER Timothy O. Bakke
MANAGING EDITOR Fran J. Donegan
ART DIRECTOR David Geer
PRODUCTION COORDINATOR Sara M. Markowitz

Current Printing (last digit)
10 9 8 7 6 5 4 3 2 1

Manufactured in the United States of America

Char-Broil Grilling Surf and Turf, First Edition
Library of Congress Control Number: 2011932133
ISBN-10: 1-58011-544-6
ISBN-13: 978-1-58011-544-5

CREATIVE HOMEOWNER®
A Division of Federal Marketing Corp.
24 Park Way
Upper Saddle River, NJ 07458
www.creativehomeowner.com

All photography by
Glenn E. Teitell and Glenn Moores
except as noted.

page 17: *right* courtesy Char-Broil;
page 20: courtesy Char-Broil;
page 21: courtesy Char-Broil

Planet Friendly Publishing

- ✓ Made in the United States
- ✓ Printed on Recycled Paper
  Text: 10% Cover: 10%

Learn more: www.greenedition.org

At Creative Homeowner we're committed to producing books in an earth-friendly manner and to helping our customers make greener choices.

Manufacturing books in the United States ensures compliance with strict environmental laws and eliminates the need for international freight shipping, a major contributor to global air pollution.

And printing on recycled paper helps minimize our consumption of trees, water, and fossil fuels. *Char-Broil Grilling Surf and Turf* was printed on paper made with 10% post-consumer waste. According to the Environmental Paper Network's Paper Calculator, by using this innovative paper instead of conventional papers we achieved the following environmental benefits:

Trees Saved: 36

Water Saved: 16,580 gallons

Solid Waste Eliminated: 1,051 pounds

Greenhouse Gas Emissions Eliminated: 3,677 pounds

For more information on our environmental practices, please visit us online at www.creativehomeowner.com/green

Courier Corporation, the manufacturer of this book, owns the Green Edition Trademark.

Acknowledgments

We would like to thank the home and professional cooks who have shared some of their recipes in this book. And to those who love backyard cooking, enjoy!

Montreal Jerk Ribs, page 108

Lemon & Ginger Grilled Alaskan Salmon Strips, page 37

Contents

Grilled Tenderloins with Blue Cheese Topping, page 91

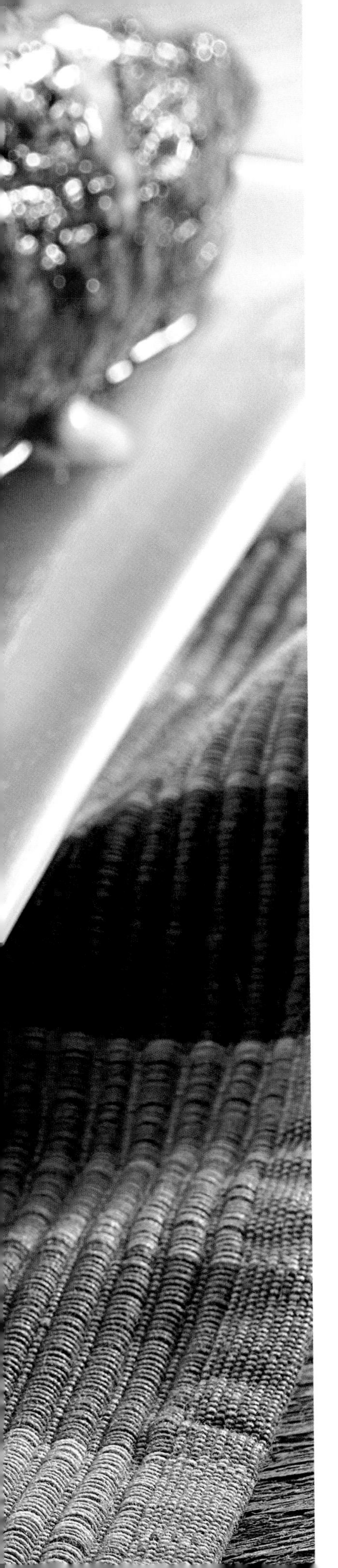

Introduction

If you love the flavor of grilled meat and seafood, feast your eyes on Char-Broil's *Grilling Surf and Turf.* This collection of flavor-sensational recipes is the answer to "What's for dinner?"

We'll get you started in Chapter 1, "Great Grillin'," by explaining how to achieve that scrumptious grilled, smoked, or barbecued flavor every time with advice from chef Barry "CB" Martin, the creator of the aptly named blog, "Sizzle on the Grill." You'll also find tips for maintaining your grill and handling food safely.

When you're ready to fire up, surf Chapter 2, "Seafood," where you'll find "Asian Salmon Burgers," page 35; "Grilled Tilapia with Sun-Dried Tomatoes," page 40; and "Cilantro-Pesto Snapper with Red Pepper Sauce," page 52, among the many mouth-watering seafood dishes.

For great-tasting beef and pork recipes, look no further than Chapter 3, "Steaks, Ribs, and Burgers." Here's the "4-1-1" on great grilled steaks, such as "CB's Rib Eyes with Balsamic-Mushroom Sauce," page 84. In the mood for ribs? Try "Kansas City Mop Ribs," page 107, which is just one example of the several tasty rib recipes in this chapter. Not to be overlooked is the classic burger. Build a better one with a recipe such as "Beer Burgers Smashed with Fresh Goat Cheese," page 115. Dee-lish!

To round out your menu, see Chapter 4, "Sides." Try "Black-eyed Pea Salad," page 121; "Grilled Potato Planks," page 126; or "Asian Super Slaw," page 138, just to name a few.

And, of course, no meal is complete without something sweet. Chapter 5, "Desserts," has that covered with lots of tempting treats, such as "Grilled Banana Splits," page 148, and "Wood-Fired Apple-Pecan Pie," page 150.

In addition, Chapter 6, "Marinades, Sauces, and Rubs," contains a variety of flavorful preparations and accompaniments that can make your main dishes and sides extra special.

Grilled Salmon Salad Vinaigrette, page 31

1 Great Grillin'

Great Backyard Cooking

GREAT BURGERS

The criteria for acclaiming a burger as "great" is regional in both flavor and style. However,my favorite is the one I enjoy with my son on any given weekend. We use coarse-ground chuck because it holds together better has great flavor.

A good fat-to-meat ratio is no more than 15 percent fat. More than that and your burgers will drip fat, shrink, and cause flare-ups—unless, of course, you are using a new Char-Broil TRU-Infrared™ gas grill, which prevents flare-ups and locks-in natural juices and flavors, giving you less meat shrinkage. Note: you can always buy a leaner ground beef and add a bit of olive oil.

Cajun Burgers, page 116

PREPPING THE PATTY. Using a wine bottle, gently press the ground chuck to about ¼ inch thick. Seasoning is a twist or two of freshly ground black pepper, a couple of pinches of coarse salt, and our "secret" ingredients: ground cumin and finely minced fresh garlic. Yeah baby—now yer talkin!

After seasoning, fold the meat, and gently press it down so it's about ½ inch thick. The seasonings are now in the middle of the patty, which evenly distributes the flavors. Use a pizza cutter to form patties out of the seasoned ground meat, making them just a bit larger than the size of the buns you plan to use. Store the patties in the refrigerator, chilling them for about 45 minutes until the grill is ready.

GRILLING RULE #1—MAKE IT HOT. Spritz the patties with a little canola oil as you take them out of the refrigerator, and put them directly on the grill to sear. I recommend a searing temperature of approximately 450°F. My new TRU-Infrared(™) grill delivers plenty of heat. The result? Juicy burgers with restaurant-quality sear marks.

After the patties sear and are no longer sticking to the grates, use a metal spatula to turn and place them on a fresh part of the grill. After grill marks are established on both sides, remove the patties to an aluminum pan or tray, cover them with foil, and allow them to finish cooking from their residual heat. I like the meat seared on the outside and pink on the inside. (The USDA recommends an internal temperature of 160°F for ground beef, pork, lamb, and veal.) When using a conventional gas grill, brush patties with melted butter instead of canola oil before placing them on the grill.

CHEESE PLEASE! While the patties are finishing, I like to add thin slices of cheese or brush the meat with BBQ sauce.

CB's Slow-Grilled Rib Eyes, page 83

SUCCULENT STEAKS

Beef cuts with marbled fat throughout the meat will cook better over direct high heat. If you prefer to grill without removing the external fat, and your steak is less than 1 inch thick, cut or notch the fat about every 3 inches to help prevent the meat from curling. If you can afford them, prime and choice grades will give you a better value for flavor and quality. (Refer to the "Guide to Basic Beef Cuts" on page 170 for an overview of the best grill cuts.)

MARINADES AND RUBS. If I pay for a good cut of beef, I want to taste the meat, not the marinade or rub. However, some grill recipes call for seasoned or marinated beef. If you must marinate, remember that the acids in citrus fruit and vinegars will break down and tenderize the meat. Marinades containing sugar will quickly burn when exposed to high temperatures. The same holds true for rubs containing sugar.

SEASONING. I recommend a light sprinkle of freshly ground black pepper and coarse salt. Some folks insist that salting a steak prior to cooking will dry it out. This is only partially true. Salt draws moisture from the steak, but that moisture is composed of naturally occurring sugars and proteins. When these are exposed to searing temperatures, they brown and form the crust so many of us enjoy at fine restaurants.

SEARING. Searing the outside of a steak at a temperature in the range of 450°F to 550°F is the way professionals do it. Make sure you don't cook the steak at this temperature for the entire time, unless you enjoy meat that is crispy on the outside and raw on the inside. (See the cooking chart on page 26.)

STEAK ON A STANDARD GAS GRILL. Most folks cook their steaks at approximately 375°F to 400°F using a traditional convection gas grill. Charcoal grills can achieve temperatures of 400°F to 450°F. It requires temperatures of at least 450°F or more—similar to the heat used in a restaurant kitchen—to see grill marks form. If your grill doesn't get this hot, lightly coat the outside of a seasoned steak with clarified butter or a touch of brown sugar.

Always turn steak with tongs or a spatula, not a fork. Check for doneness using an instant-read thermometer inserted in the side of the steak, preferably through any fat on the edge. (The USDA recommends 145°F for rare; 160°F for medium; and 170°F for well-done.)

STEAK ON AN INFRARED GAS GRILL. Set the temperature on your infrared grill to high, and place the steaks on the grill, lined up in the same direction. Cook steaks on each side for 1 to 3 minutes to sear. Remove steaks; place them in an aluminum pan or tray; cover with foil or top with another pan; and place on a cooler section of the grill to finish cooking. Check for desired doneness with an instant-read thermometer. Take note; Char-Broil TRU-Infrared(™) grills cook much faster than your traditional gas grill, so be careful not to overdo your meat.

ROASTING. Another trick you'll see in a restaurant kitchen is to pull a steak from the grill, and place it in a pan in a 400°F oven. If you try this at home, watch the internal temperature of the steak to avoid overcooking.

RESTING. After cooking, it's important to allow a steak to rest for about 10 minutes before slicing into it. This holding period keeps every bite juicy.

TENDER, MOIST PORK

Depending on the thickness, cut, and amount of fat, muscle, and bone, the cooking times for pork can vary considerably. Generally, 160°F is considered a safe internal temperature for pork and yields a much juicier piece of meat.

BRINING. Brining is similar to marinating because both methods involve soaking meat in a solution. To brine, add 1 cup of salt—and sometimes other spices—per gallon of water and soak the food for several hours or overnight. Brining makes cooked meat more moist by hydrating the cells of the muscle tissue before cooking. You can brine pork shoulders, racks, roasts, and chops.

INJECTING FLAVORS. Flavors and moisture can be added by injecting meat with marinade solutions before cooking. Needle injectors incorporate marinades directly into the thicker muscle of the meat. Here are additional tips to help you prepare pork.

➜ Use an instant-read thermometer to check the internal temperature of the meat away from the bone and nearest to the thickest part.

➜ As you reach the end of the estimated cooking time, cut into the meat near the bone to determine doneness before pulling the meat off the grill. A pork chop is cooked when the meat is no longer pink near the bone.

➜ Brush on glazes or sauces that contain sugar or honey during the last few minutes of grilling.

LIP-SMACKING PORK RIBS

There are several varieties of ribs, and each requires a slightly different technique to bring out its best flavor and texture. Here are some general rules for ribs.

➜ Apply a dry rub of herbs and spices before cooking.

➜ Cook ribs for ½ to 1 hour depending on the amount of meat, bone, and fat they contain.

➜ Baste the ribs with a light coating of apple cider vinegar during the last 10 minutes of cooking, or replace the vinegar with a glaze of marmalade or barbecue sauce.

➜ On Char-Broil's TRU-Infrared(™) gas grills, you may drop wood chips directly on or between the cooking grates. This will deliver that smoky flavor without actually smoking the ribs.

➜ Color is not necessarily an indication of when the ribs are done. Smoke from burning wood chunks can turn the interior of the meat pink. You'll know ribs are done when you can easily move the bones back and forth. To be certain, insert an instant-read thermometer into the thickest part of the meat away from the bone, measuring for an internal temperature of 160°F.

Q: "HOW LONG DO I COOK IT?" A: "UNTIL IT'S DONE."

This is the most common question I get from "Sizzle on the Grill" readers. The only honest answer I can give is that you need to learn from experience. Outdoor temperature, humidity, wind conditions, the thickness and type of meat, and the equipment you're using all factor into the finished product. Use the cooking times given in this book as a guide, and apply the USDA guidelines for safe internal food temperatures. (See chart on pages 26–27.) Remember, however, that most cuts of meat will continue to cook after they are removed from the heat, rising an additional 5 to 10°F.—CB

DELICIOUS VEGETABLES

Grilling vegetables requires little preparation and imparts a delicious, lightly smoked flavor.

➜ Set a standard gas grill to high; an infrared grill to medium-high.

➜ Lightly brush or spray vegetables with olive oil before grilling to add flavor, promote sear marks, and keep them from sticking to the grill.

➜ Some vegetables, such as corn on the cob, mushrooms, and baby eggplants, can be grilled whole. Others, such as zucchini, bell peppers, and onions, should be sliced or cut into wedges.

➜ Start vegetables over medium-high heat to sear their skins, turning every 1 to 2 minutes. Then move to low heat to finish cooking, turning occasionally.

➜ The easiest way to tell if vegetables are cooked is to pierce them with a fork or skewer. If it goes in easily, the vegetables are done.

SAVORY SEAFOOD

Grilling adds a smoky flavor to seafood and also gives it a crisp, savory crust. Whole fish, firm-flesh fish steaks and fillets, shrimp, and scallops are great on the grill. Hard-shelled mollusks, such as oysters, clams, and mussels, are often grilled in the shell, which causes the shell to open but does little to enhance the flavor.

➜ Set a standard gas grill to high; an infrared grill to medium.

➜ To prevent sticking, make sure the grill surface is clean and very hot. Use tongs to rub the grill quickly with a paper towel dipped in some oil before you add the seafood. (You can also use a grill basket or topper to grill seafood above the grill surface.)

➜ Whole fish, such as snapper, pompano, and sea bass, must be handled carefully to avoid sticking and falling apart. Firm fish steaks, such as tuna, swordfish, and shark, are particularly good on the grill because they hold together well and don't stick.

➜ Grilled shrimp are tastiest when the shell is left on. Lightly sprinkle the shrimp with salt, and grill for about 5 minutes until the shells turn pink.

GRILLED FRUIT FOR DESSERT

Lightly grilling fruit—especially stone fruits, such as peaches, nectarines, apricots, and plums—caramelizes their natural sugars, enhances their flavor, and provides appetizing grill marks.

➜ Set a standard gas grill to high; an infrared grill to medium.

➜ Generously oil grill grate to avoid sticking.

➜ Slice fruit in half, and remove pits. Grill with pulp side down, turning once, until tender, about 3 to 5 minutes.

➜ Fruit is done when it is lightly browned and tender but not mushy.

➜ Fruit can burn easily because of its sugar content, so watch it closely.

➜ Cut large fruit, such as apples, pears, mangoes, pineapples, and peaches, into chunks, and brush lightly with canola oil before grilling. Put pineapple or bananas sliced lengthwise directly on the grill.

What a Great Taste!

Many people make the mistake of over-grilling their food. To get tasty grill marks on your food, particularly meat, and still keep it moist and done-to-perfection, use the "sear and hold" technique that's practiced by professional chefs. Over direct heat, sear both sides. Then finish the food in a 350°F oven or place it on a tray loosely covered with foil, and set it on the grill away from direct heat until it reaches the desired internal temperature. That's it.

However, getting a yummy caramelized crust using a conventional gas grill can be challenging because you need very high heat (550°F to 650°F); gas flames simply don't get as hot as the hottest charcoal fire that can be banked up in a heap. So to get the grates as hot as possible, cover them with aluminum foil; turn up the heat to high; and close the lid.

Wet meat won't sear; it will steam, which isn't the way to grill a piece of meat. So while the grates are heating, blot off any moisture on the meat using a paper towel. Then spray one side of the food with a high-smoke-point oil, such as canola; open the grill lid; remove the foil; and place the meat directly on the hot grates, sprayed-side down. Check for sear marks by lifting one edge of the meat, using tongs. As soon as you see sear marks, spray the top side of the meat, and then flip it over onto a clean section of the hot grates.

When searing is done, use tongs to remove the meat to a holding tray that you can cover. Lower the heat, and allow the meat to finish at about 200°F to 300°F. Use an instant-read thermometer to check for doneness. If you want to apply a glaze, do so when the meat is fully cooked, and then place it once more directly on the hot grates for just a few seconds prior to serving.

1. Season meat with spices.

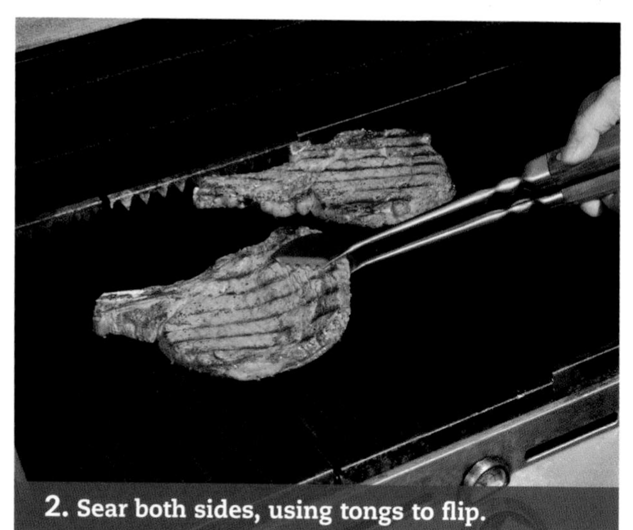

2. Sear both sides, using tongs to flip.

3. Remove to a holding tray, and cover.

4. Check internal temperature for doneness.

Smoking

Smoking is the process of cooking food between 140°F and 225°F over or near an open fire made from materials such as wood or charcoal. The fire releases particles of these materials into the smoker that impart a unique flavor to the meat. The more these materials smolder and generate smoke, the greater the number of particles to flavor the food. Cooking at temperatures of 225°F–350°F is called **HOT SMOKING.**

If the smoke passes through a cooling chamber and comes into contact with the food at a temperature of around 45°F, you are **COLD SMOKING** the food. (Note: cold-smoked food isn't actually cooked, it's simply being slow-cured and flavored.)

When moisture is added to the smoker to increase its humidity level, it is called **WET SMOKING.** A simple pan of water is placed away from direct heat inside the grill or smoker. If desired, you can use fruit juice or wine instead of water, or add these liquids to the water for an additional flavor boost.

Smoker Box (shown on top of grates for clarity)

"Smoke Bomb"

Wood Chips

Infrared Cooking

With an affordable line of *infrared* gas grills, Char-Broil has made the technology used by professional chefs for decades available to backyard grillers. You'll find it in Char-Broil's TRU-Infrared(TM) gas grills, as well as The Big Easy Oil-less Turkey Fryer and 2-in-1 Smoker, Roaster.

Infrared heat generates higher temperatures for faster cooking and uses less fuel. Preventing flare-ups, and delivering even heat with no hot spots, means much juicier foods.

So, how does it work? Infrared waves start to cook the food the instant they reach its surface, preserving the moisture barrier and quickly locking in natural juices and flavors while giving you exceptional browning.

Char-Broil's TRU-Infrared cooking system offers a wide temperature range, from a searing high heat to a low-and-slow heat for barbecuing and rotisserie grilling.

Because flare-ups are prevented, you can simply drop unsoaked wood chips on or between your grill's grates to create a slow-cooked smokehouse flavor in a fraction of the time.

TIP: TO SEAR ... OR MAYBE NOT TO SEAR

Not every cut of meat is right for searing. Cuts with a lot of connective tissue, such as beef brisket, pork shoulder, or ribs, are best slowly roasted, or barbecued, at a low temperature. This "low and slow" method of cooking literally melts the cartilage in the meat, making it juicy and tender.

Experience with your new infrared grill will help you determine what temperatures and cooking times deliver the best results. At first, you may want to adjust your regular cooking times. If you have cooked on a charcoal fire, this should be fairly easy to do. If you are more familiar with cooking on a regular convection gas grill, reduce the heat settings you normally use by at least 30 percent, and the cooking time by about 50 percent. Here are some other ideas that will help you master infrared cooking:

- ➜ Coat each piece of meat or vegetables with a light spritz of high-heat oil, such as canola.
- ➜ Plan your cooking according to technique, required times, and the best use of the grill surface.

Rotisserie Cooking

Rotisserie cooking is yet another way to roast large pieces of meat or poultry. A rotating spit driven by an electric or battery-powered motor is set directly over the heat source and turns at a constant, consistent speed to allow for even cooking. Use an instant-read thermometer inserted into the deepest part of the food to check for doneness—just be sure to stop the rotisserie motor first. It's also a good idea to wear heat-resistant gloves when you're removing the spit rod from the grill.

A rotisserie, or rotating spit, cooks large roasts over direct heat.

How to "Fry" Without Oil

The Big Easy Oil-less Turkey Fryer is a safe way to "fry" a turkey or cook rotisserie-style chicken, pork loin, roast beef or even vegetables using the same TRU-Infrared(TM) technology found in Char-Broil grills. Unlike traditional fryers, you can use your favorite dry rubs and seasonings on the meat.

1. Brine the bird up to 24 hours for extra flavor.

2. Spray cooking basket with vegetable oil.

3. Place bird—breast facing up—in the basket.

4. Allow the bird to rest for 20 to 30 minutes.

What Every Great Griller Keeps Handy

CB'S MUST-HAVE PANTRY

➜ **PURE VEGETABLE OIL/COOKING OIL SPRAY.** This is an essential tool for lubricating meat and grill grates.

➜ **COARSE SALT.** The larger crystals of coarse salt are wonderful because you can actually see where you have salted.

➜ **GARLIC** (granulated and fresh). This is a basic flavor for most grilling sauces and rubs.

➜ **CUMIN.** This spice is the secret of all great barbecue cooks.

➜ **ONIONS** (powdered, granulated, or fresh). You'll find that onions enhance most every barbecue recipe.

➜ **APPLE CIDER VINEGAR.** This provides the flavor of apple cider without the sugar and is the choice of most master grillers. Use by itself as a spray or as a liquid component of wet rubs, mops, and sauces.

➜ **KETCHUP.** This versatile ingredient can be combined with many others to form a quick sauce.

➜ **BROWN SUGAR.** I use it for dry rubs. When combined with ketchup, it creates a sweet glaze for meat. I even sprinkle a touch on steaks.

CB'S ESSENTIAL GRILLING TOOLS

➜ **KNIVES.** A good knife is essential to prepping and carving meat. I recommend you choose knives that feel good in your hand, work for different tasks, can be used outdoors, don't cost a fortune, and are easy to clean and sharpen.

➜ **SPATULA.** I've tried all styles and price points, and my favorite has a wooden handle, with a sturdy blade that supports a good-sized steak and easily slides between the grate and the food. I usually use two spatulas to remove the skin from a side of salmon during grilling.

➜ **TONGS.** I buy tongs in a variety of colors to indicate their purpose. I use red ones for raw meat and black ones for meat that's cooked.

➜ **FORK.** I primarily use the fork with the tongs and spatula when I need a little extra help. I almost never use it to poke or turn meat.

➜ **BASTING BRUSH.** I am so grateful to the person who invented silicone cooking utensils. This type of brush is my mainstay. The angle is great for getting to places without twisting my wrist, and the brush holds sauce and clarified butter quite well.

➜ **THERMOMETERS.** The most important thermometer I own is a pocket instant-read thermometer. They are very useful for quickly testing meat in various areas to see if it's cooking evenly.

Char-Broil offers a remote digital thermometer that has both a food probe and a dangling device that reads the temperature right near the grates. It alerts me if the temperature inside the smoker starts to drop, and it keeps me informed of the internal temperature of the meat.

➜ **HEAT-RESISTANT LEATHER GLOVES.** These bad boys are intended for heavy industrial use and can take sparks, heat, and hot metal. They aren't intended for playing in the fire but are very useful when you need to move hot grates and cast-iron pans, and when working around your grill, smoker, or barbecue.

How to Properly Clean Your Grill

Like most people, I'm more motivated to clean up after I finish cooking when the weather's nice. But when it's cold and dark outside, I'd rather run back into the house—balancing a plate of hot food while I dodge the raindrops—than clean the grill. Excuses, excuses. I'm just lazy sometimes. Here are a few tips and tricks I've learned over the years. Of course, be sure to check the manufacturer's directions for your grill before trying any of these.

WHY CLEAN?

If it's been a while since you last cleaned your cooking grates, here's a tip that could save you time and actually get your grates a lot cleaner. Place either a half-sheet aluminum pan or double layers of heavy-duty aluminum foil on the grates; close the lid; and turn the heat to the highest setting. (This method traps heat, causing the grill temperature to rise to between 500°F–600°F). Let the grates "cook" for about 25–30 minutes. The crud should mostly burn off and, with a light scrape from your grill brush, it all goes into the trash. Beautiful!

CHAR-BROIL BRUSH HAWG

GRILL RACKS AND GRATES

Before and after each use, you should burn off any excess grease and food that has accumulated on your grates. Turn the grill to high, and close the lid. Leave it on for around 15 minutes; this should turn most debris to ash. When grates have cooled, scrub with a cleaning brush or pad, and they should be as good as new.

STAINLESS-STEEL GRATES. Stainless-steel grates should be cleaned regularly with a heavy-duty grill brush. You can occasionally soak the grates in a mixture of water and vinegar. Periodically, remove the grates, and brush them off or lightly bang them together to remove burnt-on debris. Apply vegetable oil after cleaning to help prevent rusting.

CAST-IRON GRATES. Treat your cast-iron grates the way you would a favorite cast-iron pan. To prevent rusting, cast iron should be seasoned frequently, particularly when your equipment is new. If rust occurs, clean with a heavy brush. Apply vegetable oil or shortening, and heat to season the grates. Note: certain grills have cast-iron grates coated with porcelain. The porcelain helps prevent rust and eliminates the need for seasoning.

PORCELAIN WIRE GRATES. There are special brushes on the market, such as Char-Broil's Brush Hawg, that can clean porcelain grates without scratching. After you finish cooking, turn heat to high for approximately 5 minutes; then use the brush to clean the grates after the grill has cooled.

EXTERIOR SURFACES

For painted surfaces, warm soapy water works best. Some manufacturers offer an assortment of products for cleaning stainless-steel grills, from daily maintenance sprays and wipes to solutions that completely restore your grill's finish. Stainless-steel grills will develop rust if they are not protected from the outdoors. Check your owner's manual for detailed cleaning instructions.

Safe Food Handling—It's Basic!

I can't overemphasize the importance of good grilling hygiene. The food you serve to your family and friends must be wholesome as well as tasty. By adopting safe food-handling practices in your kitchen—and outside at your grill—you can significantly decrease your risk of food-borne illness.

KEEP IT CLEAN

Wash your hands thoroughly with hot water and antibacterial soap, especially after handling raw meat. Better yet, consider using food-safe disposable gloves—they're great for handling hot chili peppers, too. Be sure to toss them away before moving on to other tasks.

If you're using a paper towel to wipe up excess moisture from uncooked meat, dispose of it immediately when you're done. Sterilize a damp sponge in the microwave, set on high, for about 60 seconds or more until it becomes hot. Then let it cool before you grab it, or use tongs to remove it. Launder dish towels and rags in hot water.

Plastic cutting boards can be thrown in the dishwasher. Use several color-coded boards—one for raw meat, one for vegetables, one for cooked food, and so forth—to prevent cross-contamination. And don't forget to sanitize the sink. Pour diluted bleach down the drain or waste-disposal unit to kill any lingering bacteria, especially after preparing raw meat.

CB's Nut-Crusted Ribs with Bourbon Mop Sauce, page 106

Designate one cutting board for use with cooked food only.

Peanut Butter & Marshmallow Finger Sandwiches, page 145

Make this delicious dessert using grilled pound cake.

THAT GOES FOR YOUR GRILL, TOO

Burned gunk on the grates is not "seasoning." It's just old, dirty food and will add bad flavors to your next grilled meal. Take care of your grill's grates as you would a favorite cast-iron pan by preseasoning them before the first use. (See page 21 or refer to your product manual for complete instructions.)

If you don't own one of Char-Broil's infrared gas grills with a built-in self-cleaning feature, here's a secret: fold a large piece of heavy-duty aluminum foil into three layers, forming a sheet that measures about 11 × 24 inches. (A disposable foil tray works well.) Place the sheet on the grates immediately after grilling. Keep the heat turned on high on a gas grill, or lower the grates on a charcoal grill until they are just about touching the coals. The foil concentrates the heat on the grates, which helps to burn off any cooking residue. The stuff usually turns to a white ash that is easy to brush off once the grates are cool again. Follow this by spritzing the grates with a little canola oil spray to season.

Watch that Temperature

Uh, oh! Did you forget to defrost that package of burgers you were going to grill for dinner? Should you run hot water over it to thaw it quickly? What if you remembered to take the meat out of the freezer but left the package on the counter all day while you were at work?

Both of these scenarios are bad news. As soon as food begins to defrost and become warmer than 40°F, any bacteria that may have been present before freezing can begin to multiply. So, even though the center of the meat may still be frozen as it thaws on the counter, the outer layer of the food is in the danger zone. Maintain the temperature of frozen foods at under 0°F, and raw, unfrozen foods at under 40°F.

For hot foods, the minimum safe-holding temperature is above 140°F. Food can certainly pass through this temperature zone during cooking, but if it does not rise above 140°F, you are flirting with bacteria growth that will make you sick. Use an accurate meat thermometer.

As a rule of thumb, beef, pork, and most seafood should be cooked to at least 145°F; ground beef and pork should be cooked to at least 160°F.

See the cooking temperature tables and guidelines on pages 26–27 for more specific information.

You Won't Know It's Not Potato Salad, page 140

Refrigerate this salad at least 1 hr. before serving.

The Safe Way to Thaw Food

There are three safe ways to defrost food: in the refrigerator, in cold water, and in the microwave.

REFRIGERATOR THAWING

Planning ahead is the key. A large frozen roast requires at least a day (24 hours) for every 5 pounds of weight. Even a pound of ground meat needs a full day to thaw. Remember, there may be different temperature zones in your refrigerator, and food left in the coldest one will take longer to defrost.

After thawing in the refrigerator, ground meat can be chilled for an additional day or two before cooking; you can store defrosted red meat in the refrigerator for 3 to 5 days. You can also refreeze uncooked foods that have been defrosted in the refrigerator, but there may be some loss of flavor and texture.

COLD-WATER THAWING

This method is faster than refrigerator thawing but requires more attention. Place the food in a leak-proof plastic bag, and submerge it in cold tap water. Change the water every 30 minutes until the food is defrosted. Small packages of meat—about 1 pound—may defrost in an hour or less. A 3- to 4-pound roast may take 2 to 3 hours. Cook the food immediately after it defrosts. You can refreeze the cooked food.

MICROWAVE THAWING

This is the speediest method, but it can be uneven, leaving some areas of the food still frozen and others partially cooked. The latter can reach unsafe temperatures if you do not completely cook the food immediately. Foods thawed in the microwave should be cooked before refreezing.

Grill Safety

As I cruise around my neighborhood, I often notice grills on apartment terraces and backyard decks, and I get the chills. Why? Because many of these devices are way too close to wooden railings, siding, and fences. Regardless of the type of cooker you own, keep it at least 3 feet from any wall or surface, and 10 feet from other flammable objects. Here are some other tips for safe outdoor cooking from the Hearth, Patio & Barbecue Association.

→ **READ THE OWNER'S MANUAL.** Follow its specific recommendations for assembly, usage, and safety procedures. Contact the manufacturer if you have questions. For quick reference, write down the model number and customer service phone number on the cover of your manual.

→ **KEEP OUTDOOR GRILLS OUTDOORS.** Never use them to cook in your trailer, tent, house, garage, or any enclosed area because toxic carbon monoxide may accumulate.

→ **GRILL IN A WELL-VENTILATED AREA.** Set up your grill in a well-ventilated, open area that is away from buildings, overhead combustible surfaces, dry leaves, or brush. Avoid high-traffic areas, and be aware of wind-blown sparks.

→ **KEEP IT STABLE.** Always check to be sure that all parts of the unit are firmly in place and that the grill can't tip.

→ **FOLLOW ELECTRICAL CODES.** Electric accessories, such as some rotisseries, must be properly grounded in accordance with local codes. Keep electric cords away from walkways or anywhere people can trip over them.

→ **USE LONG-HANDLED UTENSILS.** Long-handled forks, tongs, spatulas, and such are designed to help you avoid burns and splatters when you're grilling food.

→ **WEAR SAFE CLOTHING.** That means no hanging shirttails, frills, or apron strings that can catch fire, and use heat-resistant mitts when adjusting hot vents.

→ **KEEP FIRE UNDER CONTROL.** To put out flare-ups, lower the burners to a cooler temperature (or either raise the grid that is supporting the food or spread coals out evenly, or both, for charcoal). If you must douse flames, do it with a light spritz of water after removing the food from the grill. Keep a fire extinguisher handy in case there is a grease fire. If you don't have one, keep a bucket of sand nearby.

→ **INSTALL A GRILL PAD OR SPLATTER MAT UNDER YOUR GRILL.** These naturally heat-resistant pads are usually made of lightweight fiber cement or plastic and will protect your deck or patio from any grease that misses the drip pan.

→ **NEVER LEAVE A LIT GRILL UNATTENDED.** Furthermore, don't attempt to move a hot grill, and always keep kids and pets away when the grill is in use and for up to an hour afterward.

Beef Cooking-Temperature Table

CUT OF MEAT	INTERNAL TEMPERATURE	VISUAL DESCRIPTION
Roasts Steaks and chops: beef	**USDA guidelines**	Depending upon how the meat is being prepared and which cut, different temperatures may be used.
medium rare	145°F	Center is very pink, slightly brown or gray toward the exterior portion
medium	155°F	Center is light pink, outer portion is brown or gray
medium well	Above 155°F	No pink
well done	Above 165°F	Steak is uniformly brown or gray throughout
Ground meat: beef, pork, lamb, veal	160°F to 165°F	No longer pink but uniformly brown or gray throughout

Pork Cooking-Temperature Table

CUT OF MEAT	INTERNAL TEMPERATURE	VISUAL DESCRIPTION
Roasts, steaks, chops	**USDA guidelines**	
	145°F	Medium-rare, pale pink center
	160°F	Medium, no pink
	160°F and above	Well done, meat is uniform color throughout
Pork ribs, pork shoulders, beef brisket	160°F and above	Depending upon how the meat is being prepared and which cut, different temperatures may be used. A pork shoulder may be prepared as a roast and would be done at 160°F, whereas the same cut when barbecued "low and slow" for pulled pork may be cooked to an internal temperature of 195°F to 200°F.
Sausage, raw	160°F	No longer pink
Ham, raw	160°F	Dark pink color throughout
Ham, precooked	Follow printed instructions	Dark pink color throughout

Seafood Cooking Temperatures and Times

FRESH OR THAWED FISH	INTERNAL TEMPERATURE	VISUAL DESCRIPTION
Salmon, halibut, cod, snapper (steaks, filleted, or whole)	145°F	Fish is opaque, flakes easily
Tuna, swordfish, marlin	145°F	Cook until medium-rare. (Do not overcook, or the meat will become dry and lose flavor.)
Shrimp	TIME COOKED	
medium-size, boiling	3 to 4 min.	Meat is opaque in center.
large-size, boiling	5 to 7 min.	Meat is opaque in center.
jumbo-size, boiling	7 to 8 min.	Meat is opaque in center.
Lobster		
boiled, whole in shell, 1 pound	12 to 15 min.	Shell turns red, meat is opaque in center.
grilled, whole in shell, 1½ pounds	3 to 4 min.	Shell turns red, meat is opaque in center.
steamed, whole in shell, 1½ pounds	15 to 20 min.	Shell turns red, meat is opaque in center.
baked, tails in shell	15 min.	Shell turns red, meat is opaque in center.
grilled, tails in shell	9 to 10 min.	Shell turns red, meat is opaque in center.
Scallops		
baked	12 to 15 min.	Milky white or opaque, and firm
seared	varies	Brown crust on surface, milky white or opaque, and firm
Clams, mussels, oysters	varies	Point at which the shell opens, throw out any that do not open

Grilling-Temperature Guidelines

METHOD OF HEAT	GRATE TEMPERATURE RANGE	DESCRIPTIVE LANGUAGE MOST OFTEN USED
Direct	Approx. 450°F to 650°F and higher	Sear, searing, or grilling on high
Direct	Approx. 350°F to 450°F	Grilling on medium
Direct	Approx. 250°F to 350°F	Grilling on low

31
34
37

42
47
50

58

63
76

2 Seafood

CB's Grilled Salmon with Shallot & Lemon Glaze

12- to-16-ounce salmon fillet

SAUCE

4 ounces anchovy fillets or paste
2 tablespoons finely chopped shallots
3 tablespoons extra-virgin olive oil
3 garlic cloves, finely chopped
½ teaspoon Worcestershire sauce
Juice from ½ lemon
3 tablespoons chopped parsley
1 tablespoon red wine vinegar
Canola oil spray

Rinse the fish under cool water, and pat dry with paper towels. Place portions in freezer to chill, but do not freeze.

Rinse and drain anchovies. Mash them in a bowl with shallots, olive oil, minced garlic, and Worcestershire sauce. Stir in lemon juice; vinegar; parsley; cover; and let stand for at least 1 hour. (If you prefer to make this ahead, chill the fish.)

Preheat grill to high. Remove fish from freezer, and spray both sides with canola oil. Place fish on grates, and sear, skin side down, about 3 to 5 minutes. Use a lightly oiled spatula to turn, and then sear the other side, about 3 to 5 minutes. Move seared fish to unheated section of grill. Brush sauce onto fish, and allow it to finish cooking. Gently insert knife into center of fillet. Fish is done when the interior is translucent and firm but not dry. Arrange fish on platter, and add more sauce if desired. ❋

Ask me what I want for dinner and I'll nearly always say, "grilled fish." Salmon is a favorite, but this recipe will work with any firm fish.—CB

Grilled Salmon Salad Vinaigrette

Rinse any ice from frozen fish under cold water; pat dry with paper towel. Preheat the grill to medium high. Brush both sides of salmon with oil. Place salmon on grill, and cook about 3 to 4 minutes until good sear marks appear. Turn salmon, and season with salt and pepper. Reduce heat to medium, and close grill lid. Cook an additional 6 to 8 minutes for frozen salmon or 3 to 4 minutes for fresh or thawed fish. Cook just until fish is opaque throughout.

Divide salad among four plates; place salmon portion on top. Drizzle with vinaigrette dressing, and serve. ❋

SALAD DRESSING

⅓ cup extra-virgin olive oil
¼ cup tarragon vinegar
1 tablespoon Dijon mustard
1 clove garlic, pressed

SALAD

4 salmon steaks or fillets (4 to 6 ounces each), fresh, thawed, or frozen
1 large apple, cored and chopped
1 ripe avocado, peeled and chopped
1 tablespoon lemon juice
1 package (10 ounces) prepared salad greens
1 navel orange, peeled and chopped
¼ medium red onion, sliced very thin
⅓ cup slivered almonds
⅓ cup raisins
2 teaspoons olive, canola, peanut, or grape-seed oil
Salt and pepper

Mix dressing ingredients in a small bowl; set aside. Place chopped apple and avocado in a large salad bowl. Drizzle with lemon juice. Add salad greens, orange, onion, almonds, and raisins; mix.

4 Servings • Prep: 20 min. • Grill: 15 min. (until interior temp. of thickest part is 145°F)

CB's Grilled Salmon with Bacon & Tomato Salsa

4 salmon steaks or fillets, approximately 6 ounces each
10 to 12 sprigs fresh thyme
2 slices thick bacon
½ cup diced red onions
1 tablespoon minced garlic
Freshly ground coarse salt and black pepper to taste
Canola, safflower, or other neutral, high-temperature oil
10 ounces (about 1 can) mild diced tomatoes with green chilies, well drained

Preheat grill to medium high. Finely chop thyme, and discard stems.

Cut bacon into ¼-inch pieces; lightly brown in a pan; and remove. Add onions to the bacon drippings, and cook until onions are sweated. Combine onions, bacon, and garlic; heat gently.

Season the salmon with salt, pepper, and thyme. Spray salmon with canola oil. Sear on both sides.

Place salmon in a foil pan on an unheated section of the grill. Close hood, and allow salmon to finish cooking until the fish is opaque in the center; the thickest part of the fish should register 145°F.

Add tomatoes to bacon mixture; simmer 4 to 5 minutes until thick. Spoon salsa over the salmon. ❋

Herbed Whole Salmon on the Grill

1 whole salmon or large salmon fillet, fresh, thawed, or frozen
4 sheets heavy-duty aluminum foil, 6 inches larger than length of salmon
1 large onion, sliced, or 2 leeks, separated into leaves
1 lemon or lime, halved
1 tablespoon preferred seasoning mix
1½ cups coarsely chopped fresh herbs (See suggested combinations of seasonings and herbs, below.)

Rinse any ice glaze from frozen salmon under cold water, and pat dry with paper towels. Lay out two sheets of aluminum foil, double thickness, on a large tray. Spray top layer with cooking spray.

Lay half of the onions or leeks lengthwise in center of the foil. Place salmon on top of onions; then squeeze lemon or lime on both sides of fish. Sprinkle dry seasoning on both sides of salmon. Place fresh herbs over, under, and—if fish is not frozen—inside the belly cavity of the fish.

Lay out remaining two sheets of foil, double thickness. Spray top sheet with oil; then place, coated side down, over salmon. Roll up, crimp, and seal all sides of foil to form a packet.

Cook salmon over medium-hot grill, 5 to 6 inches from heat, for 50 to 60 minutes if frozen; 45 to 55 minutes if fresh or thawed, turning packet every 15 minutes. Cook just until fish is opaque throughout. ❋

SUGGESTED FLAVOR COMBINATIONS

MEXICAN—lime, cilantro, onion, Mexican seasoning
MEDITERRANEAN—lemon, oregano, basil, Italian seasoning
CONTINENTAL—lemon, dill, leeks, lemon-pepper seasoning
CAJUN—lemon, onion, celery salt, Cajun seasoning

CB's Famous Smoked Salmon

Ask your fishmonger to remove pinbones from the salmon. Trim last 3 inches of the tail and belly area. Rinse the fillet under cold water, and pat dry.

Combine brown sugar, pickling salt, and contents of crab-boil bag. Add water to form a slurry that is slightly wetter in texture than paste. Place salmon fillet in a large, 2-inch-deep dish or large plastic food bag, and coat with slurry. Cover tightly with plastic wrap; refrigerate overnight. Two hours before smoking the fish, remove from refrigerator. Scrape off the slurry mixture, and place salmon into a wire strainer to drain and to save small bits of the crab boil.

Place salmon fillet flesh side up on a baking sheet; pat dry. Spread remaining bits of crab-boil seaseasoning over the fish. Carefully crisscross salmon with a very thin line of blackstrap molasses.

Allow toppings on fish to dry, using a hair dryer on low setting to speed up the process. Toppings on fish are dry when they are "tacky" to the touch.

Set your smoker for 250°F. You can add alder or cherry wood chips for extra flavor. A wet smoker is preferable for this fish; if you're using a dry smoker, keep a bowl of water in it.

Place the fish flesh side down and across the grates, so that marks run from side to side on the flesh. Close the smoker lid. Maintaining an even temperature, smoke the salmon for 1 to 2 hours—depending upon the heat of the smoke, the number of fillets, and the thickness of the fish. When fish is done, use heat-resistant gloves to remove the grate from the smoker with the fish still on it. Placing a large baking pan over the fish, turn the grate over so that the baking sheet is on the bottom. Remove the grates. Refrigerate the fish until serving time. Serve with dark bread, sliced red onions, cream cheese, lemon wedges, and capers. ❋

Salmon is high in beneficial oils, low in saturated fat and cholesterol, and easy to prepare in so many ways. This recipe produces a moist fish that makes an impressive hors d'oeuvre or appetizer. Note the 8-hour curing time.—CB

1 3- to 5-pound side of salmon, filleted, 1 inch at thickest part and 12 inches long
2 cups brown sugar
½ cup pickling salt
1 3-ounce bag crab-boil seasoning
1 tablespoon blackstrap molasses

Asian Salmon Burgers

1 pound salmon fillet, skin and pinbones removed, cut into 1-inch pieces
1 tablespoon minced ginger
1 tablespoon minced garlic
2 green onions, including 2 inches of green tops, very thinly sliced
½ tablespoon chopped fresh cilantro
1 teaspoon kosher or sea salt
1 tablespoon fresh lemon juice
½ tablespoon soy sauce
½ cup cracker meal
2 large eggs, lightly beaten

In a food processor fitted with a metal blade, pulse salmon just until coarsely ground, scraping down sides of work bowl once or twice. (Be careful; it's easy to go from chopped to mashed paste in seconds!)

Transfer salmon to a medium bowl. Add ginger, garlic, green onions, cilantro, salt, lemon juice, and soy sauce. Using a rubber spatula, mix to combine. Mix in cracker meal; add eggs. Dividing salmon mixture evenly; form into four 1-inch-thick patties. Refrigerate for at least 20 minutes before cooking. Patties can be prepared and refrigerated up to 8 hours ahead.

Preheat grill to medium. Place salmon burgers on grill, and cook for 4 to 5 minutes. Turn, and cook for an additional 4 to 5 minutes. ❋

Charred Sugar-Crusted Salmon

4 to 6 skinless salmon fillets (4 to 6 ounces each)
2 tablespoons canola oil
¼ to ⅓ cup hot Chinese-style or Dijon-style mustard, if desired

Oil a cast-iron griddle, and preheat over grill or outdoor stovetop over medium-high heat. Blend all ingredients for dry sugar rub. Generously coat one side of each salmon fillet with rub.

Carefully place salmon fillets on griddle, seasoned side down. Cook about 2 minutes to sear; turn fillets over. Reduce heat to medium, and continue cooking 6 to 8 minutes. Cook just until fish is opaque throughout.

Serve salmon over rice with mustard if desired. ❋

DRY SUGAR RUB

2 tablespoons sugar
1 tablespoon chili powder
1 teaspoon black pepper
½ tablespoon ground cumin
½ tablespoon paprika
½ tablespoon salt
¼ teaspoon dry mustard
Dash of cinnamon

Lemon & Ginger Grilled Alaskan Salmon Strips

1½ pound Alaskan salmon fillet, skin on
¼ cup canola oil
¼ cup lemon juice
2 tablespoons soy sauce
2 tablespoons honey
½ teaspoon ground ginger
¼ cup chopped green onion
1 teaspoon lemon peel

Cut salmon fillet into 1¼-inch strips. Mix canola oil, lemon juice, soy sauce, honey, ginger, green onion, and lemon peel together in a large, shallow glass dish. Add salmon strips, and coat well. Marinate 30 minutes, turning several times. Preheat grill to medium high. Remove salmon strips from marinade; discard the liquid.

Place salmon, skin side up, on grill for 3 minutes. Turn carefully, and continue to cook, skin side down, for an additional 3 to 4 minutes, or until just done and center flakes with fork. To remove strips from grill, run spatula between skin and salmon. This will provide a plate-ready, skinless strip. Garnish dish with chopped green onion, lemon peel, and lemon slices. ❋

4 Servings • Prep: 30 min. • Grill: 10 min.

North African-Style Grilled Salmon

4 salmon steaks or fillets (4 to 6 ounces each), fresh, thawed, or frozen
1 4-ounce jar green olives, drained and sliced
¾ cup low-fat plain yogurt
½ cup chopped parsley
¼ cup chopped cilantro
3 tablespoons lemon juice
2 tablespoons olive oil
1 tablespoon minced garlic
2 teaspoons paprika
1 teaspoon ground cumin
1 teaspoon turmeric
½ teaspoon salt
¼ teaspoon red pepper flakes
1½ tablespoons olive or canola oil
1 teaspoon lemon-pepper seasoning
2 tablespoons slivered red onion

Reserve 2 tablespoons of the olives. Blend remaining olives, yogurt, parsley, cilantro, lemon juice, olive oil, garlic, paprika, cumin, turmeric, salt, and pepper flakes; set aside. Rinse any ice glaze from frozen salmon under cold water, and pat dry with a paper towel. Preheat grill to medium-high.

Coat a heavy skillet with oil, and place on grill to preheat. Brush both sides of salmon with oil. Place salmon in heated skillet, and cook, uncovered, about 3 to 4 minutes, until browned. Turn salmon over, and sprinkle with lemon pepper. Cover pan tightly, and reduce heat to medium. Cook an additional 6 to 8 minutes for frozen salmon; 3 to 4 minutes for fresh or thawed fish. To serve, spoon sauce over each salmon portion, and sprinkle with reserved olives and slivered onion. ❋

Salmon Tarragon

4 salmon fillets (6–8 ounces each)
Salt and pepper
1 medium onion, diced
2 teaspoons dried tarragon
2 tablespoons chopped shallots
½ cup white wine
2 tablespoons Dijon mustard
¼ cup chicken stock
¼ cup light cream

Preheat grill to medium-high. Sprinkle salmon fillets with salt and pepper; let stand for 5 to 10 minutes.

Add remaining ingredients to medium saucepan; bring to a slow boil.

Grill salmon over medium-high heat until flesh is just opaque throughout. Drizzle with sauce, and serve. ❋

Grilled Tilapia with Sun-Dried Tomatoes

2 tilapia fillets (8 to 10 ounces each)
1 teaspoon lemon juice
Salt and pepper to taste
1 teaspoon chopped fresh cilantro
2 sun-dried tomatoes, julienned
1 medium tomato, diced
½ cup white wine
¼ red onion, diced
1 teaspoon chopped fresh parsley
¼ cup light cream

Preheat grill to medium low. Mix together lemon juice, salt, pepper, and cilantro. Pour over fish in a flat dish. In a medium saucepan, mix together all remaining ingredients except for cream. Bring to a boil; then add cream. Remove from heat. Grill tilapia 8 to 10 minutes, turning once. Place on plate; cover with sauce; and serve. ❋

Fast & Spicy Halibut

4 halibut steaks or fillets (4 to 6 ounces each), fresh, thawed, or frozen
1 tablespoon paprika
1½ teaspoons each dried oregano and dried thyme
1 teaspoon each onion powder and garlic powder
1 teaspoon each black pepper and salt
½ teaspoon cayenne pepper, or to taste
1½ tablespoons butter, melted

Preheat grill to medium high. Mix together all dry-seasoning ingredients until well combined. Rinse any ice glaze from frozen halibut under cold water; pat dry with paper towel. Place fish on a spray-coated or foil-lined baking sheet. Brush butter onto top surfaces of halibut, and sprinkle with ½ teaspoon seasoning mixture.

Grill halibut 5 to 7 inches from heat for 13 to 15 minutes for frozen halibut or 8 minutes for fresh fish. (Note: for best results with frozen fish, cook halibut 4 minutes before adding butter and spices.) Cook just until fish is opaque throughout. ❋

Grilled Halibut with a Green-Chili Blanket

4 halibut steaks or fillets, fresh or frozen (4 to 6 ounces each)
½ cup mayonnaise or plain, low-fat yogurt
1 4-ounce can mild green chilies, diced
1 tablespoon fresh lime juice
1 12 x 18-inch sheet aluminum foil
1 tablespoon chopped fresh cilantro or chives

Preheat grill to medium-high. Combine mayonnaise, green chilies, and lime juice; set aside.

Rinse any ice glaze from frozen halibut under cold water; pat dry with a paper towel. Place halibut on spray-coated foil sheet on grill. Cook 9 minutes for frozen halibut; 5 minutes for fresh or thawed fish.

Turn halibut over, and liberally spoon mayonnaise mixture onto cooked side of each portion. Sprinkle with cilantro, and cook an additional 5 to 10 minutes until fish is just opaque throughout. ❋

Recipe by Toni Bocci of Cordova, Arkansas

Thai-Style Halibut Skewers

1½ pounds boneless, skinless halibut steaks or fillets, cut into 1½ inch pieces
2 tablespoons vegetable oil
1 tablespoon Thai green curry paste
1 tablespoon freshly grated ginger
1 tablespoon rice wine vinegar
1 teaspoon nam pla (Thai fish sauce)
1 teaspoon toasted sesame oil
12 wood skewers, soaked for 30 minutes

Thoroughly blend oil, curry paste, ginger, vinegar, fish sauce, and sesame oil. Brush mixture on fish; cover; and refrigerate for 30 minutes.

Preheat grill to medium high. Thread halibut onto skewers, two to three pieces per skewer. Place skewers on well-oiled grill. Grill halibut directly above heat source for 4 to 5 minutes per side, turning once during cooking. Cook just until fish is opaque throughout. ❋

Grilled Halibut with Lemon-Caper Butter

2 halibut fillets (about ¾ pound total)
Olive oil
Salt and pepper
3 tablespoons butter
2 tablespoons capers
2 tablespoons freshly squeezed lemon juice

Here's a quick sauce for grilled fish that delivers a huge citrus punch. It's less like a lemon-caper butter than caper- and butter-flavored lemon juice.

Preheat grill to medium high. Pat the fish dry. Brush with olive oil, and season with salt and pepper on both sides. Grill halibut 5 minutes on the first side and 2 to 5 minutes on the other side, depending on the thickness of the fish.

Meanwhile, melt the butter over low heat in a small saucepan. When melted, stir in the capers and lemon juice, and season with salt and pepper. Spoon the sauce over the fish right after it comes off the grill. ❋

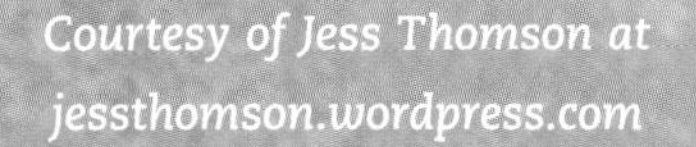

Courtesy of Jess Thomson at jessthomson.wordpress.com

CB's Thai-Glazed Swordfish

THAI GLAZE

½ cup honey
2 tablespoons soy sauce
1 tablespoon freshly grated ginger
1 teaspoon grated lime peel
1 teaspoon minced garlic
Red pepper flakes (optional)
2 tablespoons chopped basil leaves
Juice from 1 lime

2 swordfish steaks (about 6 to 8 ounces each) or other firm, white fish, such as halibut or mahi-mahi
Canola oil spray

This recipe is inspired by the delightful flavors of Thai cooking.

Mix first six glaze ingredients in a nonreactive bowl.

Preheat one side of the grill to medium high. Lightly spray fish steaks with canola oil, and place on hot grates. Sear for about 2 to 3 minutes or until sear marks appear. Lightly spray a flat, thin spatula with canola oil. Quickly slip the spatula under the fish, and turn over to a clean section of the grates to sear the other side, about 2 to 3 minutes.

When both sides are seared but fish is not quite cooked through, remove it to a holding tray away from direct heat, and brush on the glaze. Turn, and repeat on other side of fish. Fish is done when center is opaque and approximately 145°F. Place fish steaks on platter, and top with lime juice and chopped basil. ❋

4 Servings • Prep: 15 min. • Marinate: 2 hr. • Grill: 10–15 min.

Grilled Swordfish with Citrus Salsa

4 5-ounce swordfish steaks
1 tablespoon corn oil
Salt and pepper to taste

Prepare the citrus salsa—mix all ingredients except swordfish, corn oil, salt, and pepper, and let marinate for a couple of hours.

Season the swordfish steaks with salt and pepper to personal taste. Brush lightly with one tablespoon corn oil. Grill for about 5 minutes per side until fish is firm and slightly opaque. (Use a knife to check.)

Spoon the salsa over the charbroiled swordfish steaks. Garnish with mint sprigs. Great served with saffron rice, fresh asparagus, and baby carrots. ❋

CITRUS SALSA

1 ruby red grapefruit
½ orange, peeled
½ lime, peeled
1 lemon, peeled
1 medium red onion
1 cup diced red, green, and yellow bell pepper
1 tablespoon chopped cilantro
1 tablespoon chopped mint
1 ounce tequila

Section and remove white membrane from grapefruit, orange, lime, and lemon; then cut each fruit into bite-size pieces. Finely dice onion. Mix together fruit, onion, peppers, cilantro, mint, and tequila. Let salsa marinate for 1 to 2 hours before serving.

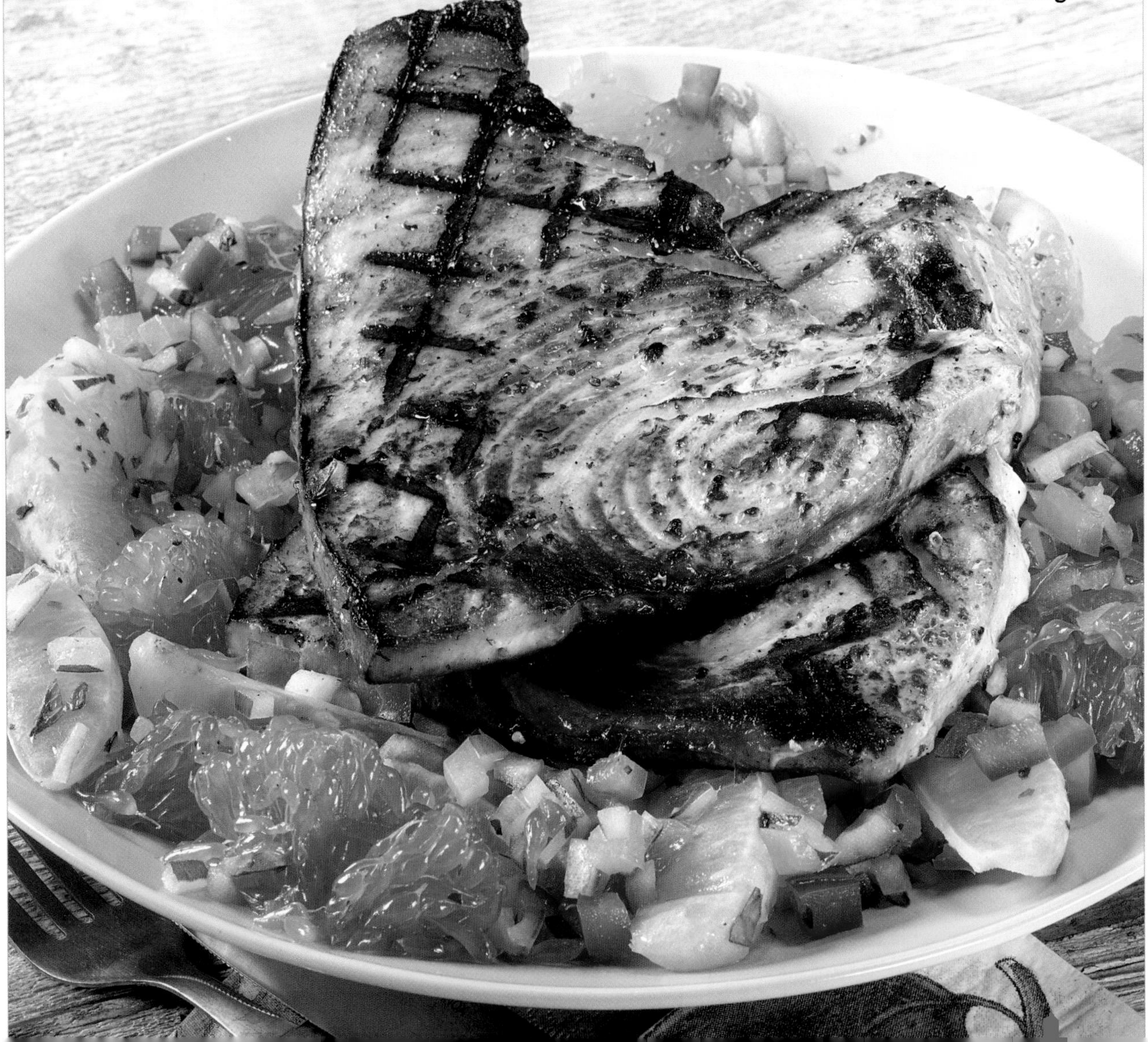

Mary's "Cape" Cod with Bacon & Leeks

16 ounces cod in 4 equal portions, skin removed
6 strips thin-cut bacon, cut into thirds
2 leeks, trimmed and sliced lengthwise
2 tablespoons minced fresh ginger
2 tablespoons minced fresh garlic
¼ cup chopped parsley
Coarse salt and ground black pepper to taste
Canola oil spray

Rinse fish under cool water, and pat dry with paper towels. Place fish in freezer to chill, but do not freeze.

In a heavy skillet, slow-fry the bacon until almost crisp; remove to drain on paper towel. When cooled, chop into large bits.

Add leeks to the pan, and sauté in the bacon fat until browned. Remove the leeks; place in bowl with ginger, garlic, bacon, and parsley; and toss to combine.

Preheat one side of the grill to high. Remove fish from freezer, and spray each side with canola oil. Place fish over hot part of grill to sear, about 3 to 5 minutes on each side. Remove fish to a holding pan on unheated side of the grill to finish cooking. Fish is cooked when the interior is flaky but not dry. Place fish on platter, and top each portion with the leek-and-bacon mixture. ❋

Grilled Cod, Yams & Plantain Skewers with Spicy Coconut Sauce

4 cod fillets (4 to 6 ounces each)
4 to 6 wooden skewers
Olive oil, as needed
Sea salt, to taste
Pepper, to taste
1 jalapeño pepper, seeded and minced
3 cloves garlic, minced
2 large, ripe, black-skin plantains or large firm bananas, peeled and cut into 1-inch slices
2 medium yams or sweet potatoes, peeled and cut into 1½-inch chunks
4 tablespoons brown sugar, divided
½ teaspoon chili powder
⅛ teaspoon nutmeg
1 14-ounce can coconut milk (regular or lite)
⅔ cup fresh lime juice
4 small green onions, thinly sliced
1 tablespoon green Thai curry paste
2 tablespoons basil cut in thin strips
1 tablespoon cornstarch
¼ cup toasted coconut

Prior to grilling, soak wooden skewers in water for 30 minutes. Brush both sides of fish fillets with olive oil, and sprinkle with salt and pepper. Score top of fillets with cuts 1½ to 2 inches apart. Mix jalapeño pepper and garlic in a small bowl. Rub mixture into cod. Cover, and refrigerate.

In large a glass bowl, microwave plantains and yams for 4 to 5 minutes on high, just until vegetables begin to soften. In separate small bowl, blend 1 tablespoon salt, 2 tablespoons brown sugar, chili powder, and nutmeg. Pour 2 tablespoons of the olive oil over vegetables; sprinkle on brown sugar mixture; stir to coat. Thread vegetables onto skewers.

Preheat grill or broiler/oven to medium high. In saucepan, blend coconut milk, lime juice, green onions, curry paste, 2 tablespoons brown sugar, basil, cornstarch, and 1 teaspoon salt until smooth. Cook on the grill or stovetop until mixture boils and thickens, stirring frequently. Keep warm.

Place vegetable skewers on the grill or broiling pan brushed with olive oil. Place cod fillets on grill rack brushed with olive oil. Cook cod and vegetable skewers 5 to 6 inches from heat for 6 to 8 minutes, turning skewers once during cooking. Cook just until fish is opaque throughout and vegetables are browned.

To serve, drizzle with ¼ cup sauce and 1 tablespoon toasted coconut. ❋

Grilled Tuna with Roasted Cipollini Onions

6 (6-ounce) tuna steaks, about 1-inch thick
2 pounds cipollini onions
⅔ cup balsamic vinegar
1 tablespoon plus ⅓ cup extra-virgin olive oil
1 teaspoon salt, plus more for seasoning
¼ teaspoon freshly ground black pepper, plus more for seasoning
3 tablespoons fresh lemon juice
2 teaspoons chopped fresh thyme leaves

If you can't find cipollini (pronounced chip-oh-LEE-nee) onions in the supermarket, you can substitute pearl onions.

Bring a large pot of water to boil. Add the onions, and cook for 2 minutes. Drain and cool. Peel the onions, and cut off the root ends.

Preheat one side of the grill to high. Toss the onions, vinegar, 1 tablespoon oil, ½ teaspoon of salt, and ¼ teaspoon of pepper in a baking dish. Close the cover, and roast over indirect heat until the onions are tender and golden, about 1 hour.

Marinate tuna in the oil, lemon juice, thyme, rest of salt, and dash of pepper, 5 minutes on each side.

Grill the steaks over direct heat to desired doneness, about 3 minutes per side for medium. Spoon the onion mixture around the tuna and serve. ❋

Courtesy of christopherranch.com

Smoky Seared Tuna Loin

1 fresh sashimi-grade tuna loin (about 3 pounds)
¼ cup soy sauce
2 tablespoons honey
Juice and zest of one lime
1 teaspoon sesame oil
1 teaspoon hot sauce
½ teaspoon ground ginger
½ teaspoon garlic powder
2 tablespoons chopped fresh cilantro
2 limes, quartered
Wood chips

Mix all of the ingredients, except the tuna, in a bowl; pour ¾ of it into a sealable plastic bag. Reserve remaining portion for sauce. Place tuna loin in bag; seal; and allow to rest in the refrigerator between 2 and 6 hours.

About 30 minutes before grilling, remove tuna from the bag; wipe off excess marinade using paper towels; and discard marinade. Return tuna to the refrigerator to air-dry, and keep chilled. (You can also place in the freezer for up to 10 minutes.)

Preheat the grill to medium high, at least 450°F, and prepare smoker box or scatter wood chips. Remove tuna from the refrigerator, and spray all sides with canola oil.

Put the tuna on the grill, and don't touch until good sear marks appear. (You can actually watch the tuna cooking by checking the sides: the meat will turn opaque and brown-beige as it cooks.) You only want to cook about ¼ inch in for rare; ½ inch in for medium. Use tongs to turn the tuna, and sear the other side.

Remove tuna to a platter, and squeeze lime juice over it. Let it rest for a couple of minutes before slicing and dressing with sauce. ❋

Our smoky seared tuna loin is a terrific summer entrée for an intimate dinner party. We start with the freshest and best tuna "tenderloin" we can buy, and then we do our best to leave it alone. Just add a simple marinade, some heat, some smoke, and WOW!—"Girls on a Grill" www.girlsonagrill.com

CB's Grilled Grouper with Garlic Butter

2 pounds grouper or black sea bass, monkfish (6- to 8-ounce portions), about 1 inch thick
3 tablespoons butter
2 cloves garlic, minced
¼ teaspoon smoked paprika
¼ teaspoon ground ginger
1 tablespoon lemon zest
1 tablespoon finely chopped fresh cilantro
Juice from ½ lemon
1½ tablespoons extra-virgin olive oil

Rinse fish in cold water; pat dry. Place fish in freezer until chilled but not frozen, about 10 to 15 minutes.

Preheat grill to high. Remove fish from freezer, and spray both sides with canola oil. Sear on both sides, about 4 to 5 minutes each. Use a lightly oiled spatula to turn.

Place seared fish in a holding pan away from direct heat to finish. Fish is done when flaky and opaque.

Combine butter, garlic, paprika, ginger, and lemon zest in saucepan over medium heat until the aromas are released; do not brown the garlic. Reduce heat, and add cilantro, lemon juice, and olive oil; then remove from heat. Spoon the garlic butter sauce over the fish.

An alternative method is to baste the fish while cooking to add a tasty glaze. However, if you are not experienced with grilling fish, the original method works well. ❋

Cilantro-Pesto Snapper with Red-Pepper Sauce

4 snapper or mahi-mahi or swordfish fillets (1½ pounds)
2 tablespoons shredded Parmesan cheese
2 fresh garlic cloves
⅓ cup chopped walnuts
1 tablespoon extra-virgin olive oil
¼ cup fresh cilantro
¾ teaspoon pepper, divided
1 medium shallot
½ cup white wine
1 (12-ounce) jar roasted red peppers, drained
¾ teaspoon salt, divided
1 tablespoon butter

Preheat grill to medium high. Make pesto: place cheese, garlic, and walnuts in food processor; process 15 to 20 seconds or until finely chopped. Add olive oil, cilantro, and ⅛ teaspoon of the pepper. Process until smooth; remove from food processor, and set aside.

Mince shallot finely; combine with wine in saucepan. Bring to boil; reduce heat to medium, and cook about 4 minutes, stirring occasionally, or until liquid has reduced by about one-half.

Put red peppers in a food processor; add wine reduction; and process 20 seconds or until smooth. Pour mixture back into the same pan, and bring to a boil; reduce and simmer 3 to 4 minutes, stirring often, or until sauce thickens.

Season fish with ½ teaspoon of the salt and ¼ teaspoon of the pepper. Grill fish with the lid closed about 4 to 6 minutes on each side or until fish is golden and separates with a fork.

Add butter to sauce, along with remaining salt and pepper; whisk until smooth. Spoon sauce onto serving plates containing yellow rice and peas; place fish on sauce; and top with pesto. ❋

CB's Snapper Grilled on a Bed of Limes

2 snapper fillets or other delicate fish
3 large limes, very thinly sliced
2 teaspoons butter, melted, per fillet
Smoked paprika for seasoning and color
Canola oil spray

Preheat the grill to medium high. Carefully rinse the fish, and pat dry with paper towels. Spray one side of the lime slices with canola oil, and arrange them in the center of the grill to form a "bed" for each fillet.

Lay the fish atop the lime slices, and baste with melted butter and a generous pinch of smoked paprika. Lightly tent the fish fillets with heavy-duty aluminum foil, or cover each with a small foil pan. Reduce the heat to medium, and allow the limes to char and release their juices to flavor the fish.

Check the fish after about 10 to 15 minutes. When fish is opaque and firm to the touch, slip a lightly oiled spatula beneath the limes and lift the fish off the grill. Serve fish on individual plates, and garnish with parsley if desired. ❋

This is an easy, flavorful method for grilling snapper, sole, or any thin fish fillets, which tend to fall apart on a hot grill.—CB

2 Servings • Prep: 15 min. • Chill: 2 hr. • Grill: 10 min.

CB's Baja-Style Grilled Sea Bass

1 whole sea bass or other firm-flesh fish, such as snapper or trout (about 2 pounds), head and fins removed
½ cup achiote paste (usually found in the Mexican food section of the supermarket)
½ cup orange juice
3 tablespoons lemon juice
3 tablespoons lime juice
Salsa to garnish

Ask your fishmonger to dress and butterfly the fish. Rinse the fish, and pat it dry. Use a sharp knife to score the skin lightly. Spread a mixture of achiote paste and the citrus juices over the inside of the fish, avoiding the skin. Refrigerate for at least 2 hours.

Preheat the grill to medium. Spritz the skin of the fish with canola oil; place it, skin side down, on the grill. Tent the fish with heavy-duty aluminum foil, shiny side facing the fish, taking care not to let the foil touch the fish, or cover with a disposable aluminum tray.

Cook the fish until the fish juices and seasonings begin to steam and the flesh of the fish is firming up to your desired taste. Serve with a lightly sweet salsa. ❋

Serve with Creamy Zucchini & Garlic, page 136; and Pineapple Salsa, page 139

Grilled Bluefish with Fresh Corn Salsa

- 4 bluefish fillets (6 to 8 ounces each)
- Salt and black pepper, to taste
- 3 ears fresh or frozen corn, kernels removed
- 6 sprigs fresh cilantro, roughly chopped
- 2 teaspoons finely diced red onion
- 1 jalapeño, seeded and finely chopped
- Juice of 2 limes
- 1 pinch cumin
- 1 teaspoon canola oil

TO MAKE SALSA: mix all vegetables and spices together in a nonreactive bowl. Toss; cover for at least one hour.

Preheat grill to medium high. Brush fillets with oil. Cook fish for 2 to 3 minutes on each side. Remove from grill, and place in 225°F oven for 3 to 5 minutes. While fillets are in the oven, heat skillet until it is hot; add salsa; and cook approximately 2 minutes or until all ingredients are warm. Remove from heat. Arrange fish on plates, and garnish with salsa. ❋

Maryland Smoked Bluefish

2 pounds bluefish fillets or 3 pounds bluefish steaks
1 cup salt
1 gallon water
1 pound hardwood chips (whichever type you prefer)
¼ cup neutral-flavored vegetable oil or clarified butter

Dissolve salt in 1 gallon of water to make the brine. Marinate fish in brine for 30 minutes.

Preheat grill to low, and set up for indirect heat. Place smoker box filled with dry wood chips (alder, apple, or pear work well) directly over the heat source.

Remove fish from brine; rinse in cool water; and pat dry with paper towels. If possible, allow fish to dry in the refrigerator for up to 1 hour.

Brush grate where fish will cook with oil. Place fish, skin side down, on unheated side of grill. If your grill doesn't have a thermometer, center an oven thermometer at the back of grill. Maintain temperature of 200–250°F.

Brush top of fish with oil. Close grill cover, and smoke fillets or steaks about 30 to 45 minutes (for whole fish, about 45 minutes). If the surface of the fish dries out a bit, baste with clarified butter or vegetable oil during the final 10 minutes of cooking.

The fish is done when its flesh is opaque and firm. Serve with chopped hard-boiled egg, chopped onion, capers, and toast triangles. ❋

Cajun Grilled Mahi-Mahi with Avocado Salad

4 fillets of mahi-mahi (4 ounces each)
1 tablespoon canola oil
1 tablespoon Cajun seasoning
2 large, ripe avocados, peeled and diced
1 cup cooked corn kernels
1 16-ounce can black beans, drained and rinsed
¼ cup diced red onion
1 medium tomato, diced
1 medium green bell pepper, diced
2 tablespoons chopped fresh cilantro
1 tablespoon minced jalapeño (optional)
¼ cup olive oil
2 tablespoons lime juice
½ teaspoon cumin
Salt and pepper to taste

Preheat grill to medium high. Brush the fillets with the oil, and sprinkle both sides with Cajun seasoning. Grill for about 4 to 5 minutes on each side, until the fish is cooked to your desired doneness and nicely browned.

Meanwhile, combine the avocado, corn, black beans, red onion, tomato, bell pepper, cilantro, and jalapeño in a bowl. Stir together olive oil, lime juice, and cumin, and add to salad. Season to taste with salt and pepper, and toss.

Top each fillet with some of the avocado salad, and serve immediately. ❋

CB's Rainbow Trout Stuffed with Lemon, Shallots & Herbs

2 12- to-14-inch rainbow trout, cleaned (head and tail removed if desired)
Salt and freshly ground pepper
2 tablespoons minced shallots
2 small lemons, sliced very thin
1 bunch dill, divided
1 bunch tarragon, divided
Canola oil spray
Seasoned wood chips, if desired

Preheat grill to high. Season the cavity of each fish with salt and pepper; add 1 tablespoon of shallots to each; and rub all ingredients into the fish. Add lemon slices, dill, and tarragon. Secure stuffing by wrapping fish with kitchen twine or sealing with toothpicks if necessary.

Spray skin of each fish with canola oil. Place fish in grill basket and close.

Reduce heat of grill to medium. Place fish basket on the grill, and cover with a piece of aluminum foil to retain heat and moisture. Close hood, and cook for approximately 5 to 7 minutes. Lift basket off grill to check for grill marks; turn basket; and grill on other side, about 5 to 7 minutes.

Remove basket, and place it in a pan to allow the fish to rest for a few minutes. Using two spatulas to support the fish on each end, remove from the basket, and place on a plate.

To debone fish, insert the tip of a sharp boning knife into the top of the fish and "feel" your way to the spine. Run the knife gently along the spine toward the tail. Use two forks to lift off this half of the fish; then pinch the top end of the spine with two fingers, and peel it away from the bottom half of the fish. Replace the top half.

For a quick sauce, briefly sauté thin lemon slices with pinches of the tarragon and dill in a touch of butter and olive oil until the lemon releases its aroma. Drizzle over each fish serving, and place a lemon slice on top. ❋

Trout is available nearly year-round in just about every market. This recipe is easy because I use a fish basket to hold the stuffed fillets—it makes turning a breeze.—CB

Grilled Chesapeake Croaker

4 whole croaker or other lean, white fish, dressed
¼ cup soy sauce
2 tablespoons brown sugar
1 clove garlic, minced
1 tablespoon freshly minced ginger
2 tablespoons finely julienned orange peel
2 tablespoons orange juice
¼ teaspoon crushed red pepper flakes
2 tablespoons melted butter
4 scallions, sliced

Atlantic croakers are usually caught in the Chesapeake Bay between June and August. Also known as "hardhead," croakers contain delicate white meat with a sweet flavor that ranges from mild to moderately pronounced. You can substitute croaker for any recipe that calls for catfish, perch, sea trout, spot, or striped bass.

Place fish in a bowl. Combine remaining ingredients, and pour over fish. Marinate for one hour in the refrigerator. Preheat grill to medium. Place fish on grill, about 5 inches from heat, and cook about 10 minutes per inch of thickness, turning once halfway through cooking time and basting often with the marinade. When fish is tender and flakes easily, remove from grill, and serve hot over fresh corn salsa. (See page 55 for recipe.) ❋

4 Servings • Prep: 20 min. • Marinate: 1 hr. • Grill: 6 min.

Hawaiian-Style Marlin with Poke Sauce

16 ounces fresh marlin cut into 4 portions, about 1 inch thick
2 teaspoons finely minced fresh ginger
1½ cups soy sauce
1 tablespoon brown sugar
½ teaspoon sesame oil
2 tablespoons chili oil
Shredded Napa cabbage (garnish)
Cooked white rice

Combine ginger, soy sauce, brown sugar, sesame oil, and chili oil in a small bowl. Place the fish in a resealable plastic bag; pour in the marinade; seal bag; and let rest in refrigerator for up to 1 hour.

Mix poke sauce ingredients in a blender or by hand until emulsified. Refrigerate until ready to use.

Preheat the grill to high. Remove fish from bag, and discard the marinade. Place fish on the grill, and sear one side, about 2 to 3 minutes. Use a lightly oiled spatula to turn and sear the other side, about 2 to 3 minutes. Remove, and plate.

The marlin will be seared on the surface and very rare in the middle. Serve garnished with chopped Napa cabbage, white rice, and ramekin of poke sauce. ❋

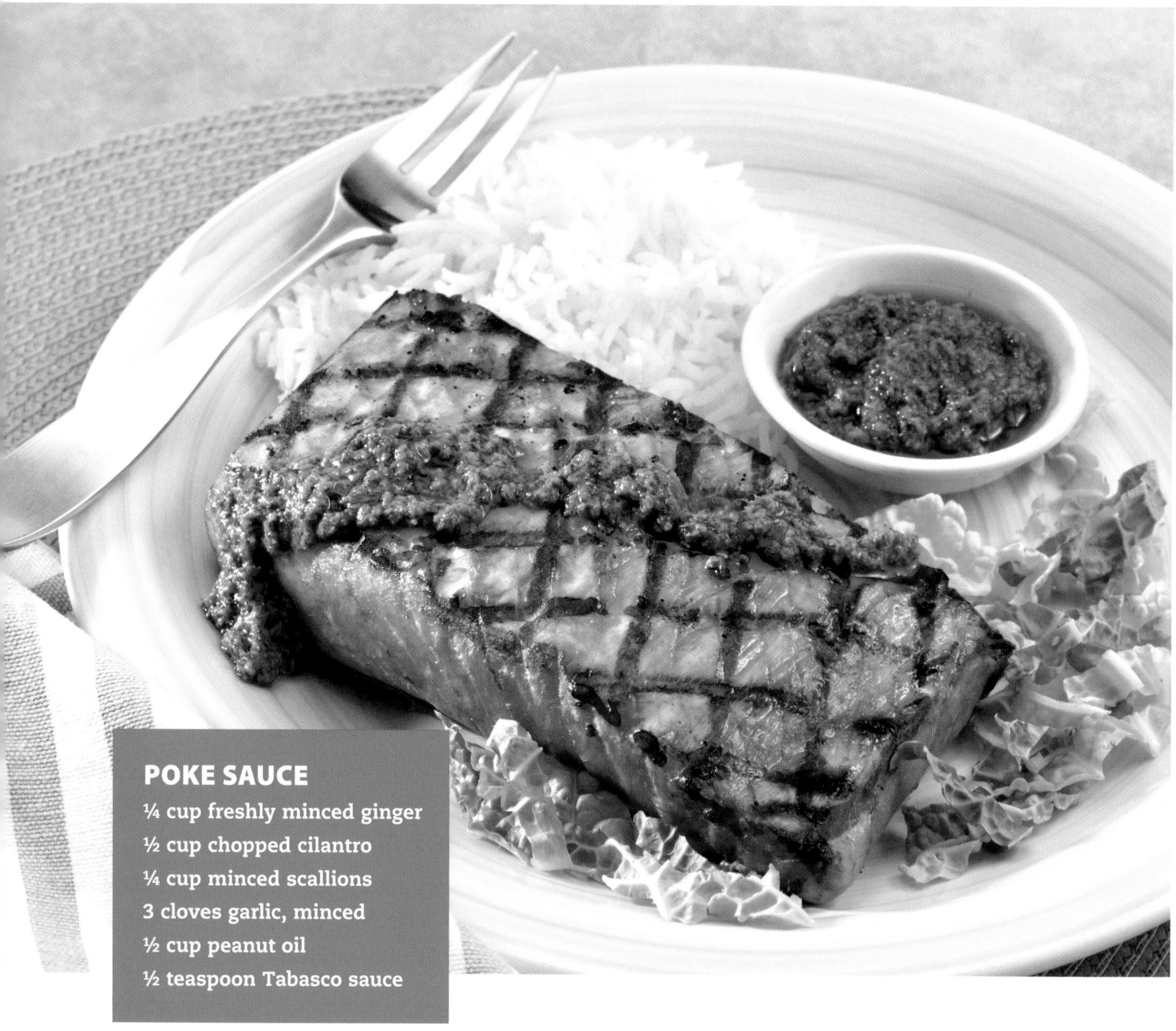

POKE SAUCE

¼ cup freshly minced ginger
½ cup chopped cilantro
¼ cup minced scallions
3 cloves garlic, minced
½ cup peanut oil
½ teaspoon Tabasco sauce

Margarita Grilled Shrimp

1½ pounds shrimp, peeled and deveined
¼ cup vegetable oil
3 tablespoons fresh lime juice
3 tablespoons tequila
2 tablespoons triple sec
1 large jalapeño chili, seeded and minced
1½ teaspoons grated lime zest
1 teaspoon chili powder
½ teaspoon coarse salt
1 teaspoon sugar

Whisk all ingredients together, except shrimp, in a medium-size bowl. Allow the mixture to rest for at least 20 minutes. This marinade can be prepared 1 day in advance. Simply cover and refrigerate for up to 24 hours.

Pour about ¼ cup of the marinade mixture into a container, and reserve. Place shrimp in a large baking dish or sealable plastic bag, and cover with remaining marinade. Cover dish with plastic wrap, or seal bag and refrigerate shrimp for 30 minutes.

Remove shrimp from container, and discard marinade. Grill shrimp on indirect heat for 3 to 4 minutes per side, basting with the reserved marinade. Serve over rice. ❋

6 Servings • Prep: 20 min. • Marinate: 2 hr. • Grill: 10–15 min. combined

Chipotle Shrimp

1½ pounds uncooked jumbo shrimp, peeled and deveined
2 teaspoons olive oil
1 cup finely chopped onion
4 garlic cloves, minced
2 teaspoons ground cumin
1 teaspoon dried oregano
1 cup water
¼ cup apple cider vinegar
2 teaspoons chopped canned chipotle chilies
¼ cup orange juice
2 teaspoons light brown sugar

Heat oil in heavy skillet over medium heat. Add onion; sauté for about 10 minutes or until golden brown. Add garlic, cumin, and oregano; stir 1 minute. Transfer mixture to blender. Add water, vinegar, and chipotles to blender; puree until smooth. Transfer half of puree to medium bowl; cool. Add shrimp to bowl, and toss to coat. Cover; chill 2 hours.

Pour remaining puree into heavy medium saucepan. Add orange juice and brown sugar; bring to a boil. Reduce heat; simmer for about 10 minutes or until glaze is slightly thickened and reduced to ½ cup. Remove from heat, and cool.

Preheat grill to medium high. Remove shrimp from marinade; pat dry using paper towels. Lightly brush shrimp with orange juice glaze. Grill shrimp, brushing once more with marinade, until shrimp are opaque in center, about 2 minutes per side. Transfer to platter. ❋

Grilled Shrimp & Vegetable Kebabs

2 pounds shrimp, peeled and deveined
4 to 6 wooden skewers
2 medium zucchini, cut into ½-inch half-rounds
2 medium yellow squash, cut into ½-inch half-rounds
1 medium onion, cut into ½-inch pieces

MARINADE

2 garlic cloves, minced
1 tablespoon chopped fresh oregano
2 teaspoons lemon juice
1 teaspoon lemon zest
¼ cup olive oil

These shrimp kebabs are a tasty main dish when paired with rice or another grain. At a casual gathering, guests can even assemble and grill their own kebabs.

Soak the skewers in water for 20 minutes. For the marinade, whisk together the garlic, oregano, lemon juice, zest, and oil.

Thread each skewer with alternating shrimp and vegetables. Place the skewers in a large baking dish, and pour the marinade over them. Turn the skewers to coat with the marinade, and refrigerate up to 1 hour.

Preheat one side of the grill to high. Lightly spray the hot side of grill with vegetable oil.

Shake any excess marinade off the skewers, and place them on the hot side of the grill. Leave them alone to brown on the one side, a minute or so. Turn skewers, and brown the vegetables on all sides until the shrimp is cooked, about 4 to 6 minutes. ❋

Courtesy of www.cookthink.com

Bob & Lee's Rosemary & Garlic Grilled Shrimp

1 pound raw shrimp, peeled, tails on
1 clove garlic, minced or chopped
1 teaspoon crushed dried rosemary, or 2 teaspoons finely chopped fresh rosemary
1 teaspoon dried basil, or 2 teaspoons finely chopped fresh basil
1 teaspoon freshly ground pepper
⅛ teaspoon kosher or sea salt
1 to 2 teaspoons extra-virgin olive oil

Marinating time can be overnight if preparing on a stove or 1 hour before grilling.

Mix first five ingredients together in a large bowl; marinate shrimp in refrigerator 1 hour or overnight. Preheat grill to medium heat. Just before grilling, add salt and 1 to 2 teaspoons of extra-virgin olive oil to shrimp mixture; mix to coat well.

Place shrimp on grill, and cook for 3 minutes on each side. Serve. ❋

Thai Shrimp

15 to 20 shrimp, tails on
1 tablespoon Cajun spice mix
1 cup white wine
1 teaspoon chopped fresh cilantro
1 teaspoon Tabasco sauce
½ teaspoon chili paste
½ teaspoon lime juice
1 pinch of chili flakes

Preheat grill to medium high. Place shrimp in medium-size bowl. Sprinkle Cajun spice on shrimp, and toss until lightly coated. Add remaining six ingredients to medium saucepan.

Grill shrimp over medium-high heat, turning once, for 4 to 5 minutes or until pink. Place saucepan containing sauce ingredients over heat. Place shrimp in sauce; bring to a boil for about 2 minutes. Serve. ❋

10 Servings • Prep: 30 min. • Marinate: 1 hr. • Grill: 5 min.

Grilled Shrimp & Blue Cheese Grits

5 pounds shrimp, peeled and deveined with tail on
¼ cup olive oil
¼ cup soy sauce
¼ cup white wine
2 teaspoons Cajun seasoning or seasoned salt
5 pounds assorted vegetables (peppers, zucchini, onions, mushrooms)
½ cup olive oil
¼ cup sliced fresh basil
Salt and pepper, to taste
4 cups stone-ground grits
1 cup crumbled blue cheese
10 skewers

Combine oil, soy sauce, wine, and Cajun seasoning. Add shrimp. Refrigerate and marinate for 1 hour. While the shrimp marinate, dice or julienne the vegetables. Heat a pan over high heat; add oil; and sauté vegetables until softened, about 5 minutes. Add basil, and remove from heat. Season vegetables with salt and pepper.

Cook grits following package directions, about 20 minutes. Add blue cheese, and simmer until thick. Cover to keep warm.

Preheat grill to high. Skewer shrimp, and place on grates. Cook until just opaque, turning once, about 5 minutes. To serve, place grits in center of platter. Top with vegetables. Surround with shrimp. ❋

Jim "Houston" Hatcher's Creole Shrimp & Sausage

1 pound Andouille sausage
1 pound jumbo Gulf prawns (about 23 per pound), cleaned
Canola oil

CREOLE SAUCE

⅓ cup Creole or stone-ground mustard
1 tablespoon orange marmalade or preserves
2 teaspoons Tabasco sauce

Combine sauce ingredients, and set on grill away from direct heat to warm.

Preheat one section of grill to high and one section to low. Sear the sausages on the hot side of the grill, and move to a pan on the low side to finish.

When the sausages are just about done (160°F internal temperature), spray the prawns with canola oil, and place over direct heat to sear. When grill marks appear, remove them to the pan with the sausages. Add the Creole sauce to coat the prawns and sausages; serve with mac and cheese (page 132) or over white rice. ❋

3–4 Servings • Prep: 1 hr. • Marinate: 1 hr. • Grill: 7–10 min.

CB's Grilled Honey & Lime Gulf Prawns

1 pound jumbo Gulf prawns (about 21 per pound) cleaned, tails on

Combine marinade ingredients in a sealable plastic bag, and add Gulf prawns. Refrigerate for up to 1 hour. Combine basting-sauce ingredients in a nonreactive bowl, and set aside.

Preheat grill to medium high. Place marinated prawns on hot grates. Use tongs to turn, and sear all sides. When seared, remove the prawns to a holding pan away from direct heat. Brush with basting sauce, and allow to finish cooking, about 3 to 5 minutes. Prawns may be served as a main course over rice or pasta or with a salad, such as "You Won't Know It's Not Potato Salad," page 140. ❋

MARINADE

2 tablespoons Italian salad dressing
2 tablespoons dry white vermouth
⅓ cup Worcestershire sauce
1 garlic clove, finely minced
2 tablespoons finely chopped cilantro
1 teaspoon ground ginger

BASTING SAUCE

2 tablespoons Worcestershire sauce
¼ cup olive oil
¼ cup honey

Garlic-Lime Alaska Prawns with Avocado Cream

1½ pounds peeled Alaska Spot Prawns, or large shrimp, tails on
1½ tablespoons kosher salt
1½ tablespoons sugar
¼ cup olive oil
¼ cup chopped fresh cilantro
3 cloves garlic, peeled and minced
2 teaspoons grated lime peel
½ teaspoon fresh-ground pepper
Wooden or metal skewers
Avocado Cream (See recipe on page 161.)

In a bowl, combine salt and sugar. Rinse prawns; pat dry. Add prawns to salt-sugar mixture; stir gently to coat. Cover, and refrigerate for up to 1 hour.

Rinse prawns well, and drain. Preheat grill to high. In another bowl, combine olive oil, cilantro, garlic, lime peel, and pepper. Add prawns, and mix to coat. Thread prawns on metal or soaked wooden skewers, running them through each prawn at the tail and head to form a C-shape.

Lay skewers on well-oiled grill grates. Close lid on grill. Cook, turning once, just until prawns are opaque throughout, about 3 to 5 minutes total. Slide prawns off skewers, and arrange on platter. Set avocado cream alongside.

Note: a brief cure in salt and sugar adds flavor to prawns and makes them more tender. You can cure and marinate the prawns up to 1 day ahead. Chill in an airtight container. ❋

Prawns with Parmesan-Herb Baste

24 Alaska Spot Prawns or jumbo shrimp, peeled, tails on
12 wooden skewers
¼ cup freshly grated Parmesan cheese
2 tablespoons olive oil
2 tablespoons red wine vinegar
1½ teaspoons dried basil
1 teaspoon coarsely ground black pepper

Soak skewers in water for at least 30 minutes. Blend grated cheese, olive oil, vinegar, basil, and pepper. Place two prawns on each skewer, carefully piercing through both head and tail sections. Transfer skewers to baking tray; brush each prawn with parmesan mixture; cover and refrigerate for 30 minutes. Reserve any remaining baste.

Preheat grill to medium-high. Place skewers directly over heat on well-oiled grill; cook for 3 to 4 minutes. Turn once; brush with remaining baste; and continue to cook for 3 to 4 minutes or until prawns turn pink and are opaque throughout. ❋

Lobster Tails with Brown Sugar Sauce

4 lobster tails
3 tablespoons brown sugar
¼ cup butter
¼ cup breadcrumbs

DIPPING SAUCE

¼ cup butter
2 cloves garlic, crushed
1 teaspoon chopped parsley
Salt and pepper

Combine lobster, brown sugar, butter, and crumbs in a small saucepan. Place pan over medium heat, stirring occasionally, until butter is melted and sugar is dissolved.

Preheat grill to medium. Cook lobster tails on grill for 4 to 6 minutes.

In a separate saucepan, combine ingredients for dipping sauce. Heat until butter is melted. Remove lobster from grill, and baste with lobster mixture. Serve with dipping sauce. ❋

CB's Grilled Lobster Tail with Bourbon-Herb Sauce

2 lobster tails removed from shell, about 6 ounces each
Canola oil

SAUCE

5 tablespoons butter, melted
1 tablespoon olive oil
¼ cup finely diced shallots
1 garlic clove, finely minced
Coarse salt and freshly ground black pepper to taste
¼ cup Kentucky bourbon
1 tablespoon finely chopped chives
1 tablespoon finely chopped tarragon
2 tablespoons dry white vermouth

Melt butter in a heavy saucepan over medium heat. Add olive oil and shallots, and cook until translucent; stir in garlic, and heat until aroma is released. Add salt and pepper to taste. Add bourbon; allow alcohol to vaporize; remove from heat; and set aside, covered.

Preheat grill to medium high. Dry lobster with paper towel, and then lightly spray with canola oil. Place lobster tails on hot grill to sear, using tongs to turn. When seared, remove to an aluminum pan away from direct heat, and continue to cook until lobster is firm but not rubbery, about 15 minutes.

Prior to serving, add the chives, tarragon, and vermouth to the sauce; re-warm to release the flavors. Serve on plates with sauce drizzled over the lobster or as a dipping sauce. ❋

CB's Grilled Sea Scallops with Lemon & Fennel Sauce

10 large sea scallops, fresh or thawed
1 large lemon with unblemished peel
2 egg yolks
2 teaspoons canola oil, or cooking oil spray
1 medium-large fennel bulb, sliced lengthwise and cut into bite-size strips
1½ cups dry white wine, champagne, or dry vermouth
1 cup unsalted chicken broth
⅛ teaspoon cinnamon or nutmeg
½ tablespoon corn starch
2 teaspoons sea salt or kosher salt
2 teaspoons freshly ground black pepper

Using a citrus zester or grater, zest the lemon rind. Juice remainder of lemon, and reserve.

In a small bowl, add egg yolks and about 1 tablespoon of lemon juice. Mix using a whisk—do not froth.

Preheat oven to medium high. In a medium-size saucepan, add 1 tablespoon of canola oil. Add fennel, and heat slightly; then add wine and lemon zest. Bring mixture to a boil; cook until reduced by half. Blend in broth and nutmeg or cinnamon. Return to boil; then reduce heat to medium. Cook until sauce is reduced by about half.

Add some of the sauce reduction to the egg-and-lemon-juice mixture; stir; then add the rest. Continue to cook on medium heat until creamy. If sauce is not coming together, add a very small amount of cornstarch. Add lemon juice and sea salt to taste.

Preheat grill to medium high. Spray scallops with cooking oil; grill for about 3 minutes; then turn, placing scallops on another section of grates for approximately 3 minutes. Remove to a covered dish and set aside. Ladle a generous portion of sauce on each plate, and top with three to five scallops. ❋

Scallops can be seared on cast-iron grates when using a charcoal or gas grill. If you have one of the new Char-Broil infrared grills, use a medium-high setting.—CB

CB's Grilled Scallops with Asparagus & Toasted Walnuts

1 dozen sea scallops, cleaned and dried with a paper towel
3 large walnut halves or 6 large hazelnuts, chopped
1 pound asparagus, woody ends removed
Salt and pepper to taste
Juice from ½ lemon
Soy sauce

To toast nuts, place them in a dry skillet over medium-low heat, shaking pan to prevent burning, for about 2 to 3 minutes until aroma is released. When cool, chop nuts, and set aside.

Preheat the grill to medium. Spray the scallops and asparagus with canola oil, and season with salt and pepper to taste. Place asparagus on the grill, and use tongs to turn until all sides are charred and spears are tender, about 4 to 5 minutes. Remove to serving plate, and lightly cover with foil. Use tongs to place the scallops on a clean section of the grill. Leave in one place until seared; use tongs to turn the scallops; and sear the other sides. Remove, and place atop seared asparagus. Serve with a mixture of equal parts fresh lemon juice and soy sauce. Garnish with lemon zest and chopped nuts. ❋

CB's Grilled Soft-Shell Crabs

8 soft-shell crabs, cleaned
Coarse salt and pepper to taste
Canola oil spray
1 lime cut into quarters

SAUCE

2 cloves minced garlic
1 tablespoon minced ginger
1 chipotle pepper, finely diced
3 tablespoon canola oil
1 teaspoon anchovy paste
1 cup finely chopped fresh cilantro
1 cup finely chopped Thai basil

Combine all sauce ingredients, and set aside.

Preheat the grill to high. Season the crabs with salt and pepper to taste; spritz with canola oil; place on clean grates; and sear on both sides—about 3 minutes per side—using tongs to turn.

Remove crabs, and place them on a platter where the sauce is spread as a base. Squeeze limes over grilled crabs; then spoon sauce over the crabs, and serve. ❋

Smoky Grilled King Crab

Wood chips, alder, cedar, apple, etc. (2 to 3 pounds)
Alaska King Crab legs, frozen
2 to 3 tablespoons olive oil
2 to 3 teaspoons favorite seafood spice blend
1 large-size foil cooking bag or 2 sheets (15-inch) heavy-duty aluminum foil

Soak wood chips in water for 30 minutes; drain. Preheat grill to medium high. Add chips to grill or smoker box.

Rinse crab legs under cold water to remove any ice glaze; pat dry with paper towels. For each pound of crab, use 1 tablespoon olive oil and 1 teaspoon of seafood spice. Blend olive oil and seasoning. Place foil bag in a 1-inch-deep baking pan. Place crab legs in bag. Pour or brush oil blend onto legs; seal the bag tightly. If using foil sheets, place crab legs on the foil, and pour or brush oil blend onto legs. Lay second foil sheet over crab, and tightly crimp edges to seal foil, leaving room for heat circulation inside.

To cook, slide bag onto grill, and cook for 8 to 10 minutes, until the internal temperature of the crab reaches 145°F. (Use an instant-read thermometer, and test crab for doneness in shoulder section.) ❄

Grilled Alaska Crab with Trinidad Salad

⅓ cup butter, melted
¼ to ½ teaspoon chili oil
⅛ teaspoon cayenne pepper
3 to 4 pounds Alaska Crab legs (King, Snow, or Dungeness), split open to expose meat

In a small bowl, whisk together olive oil, one-half of the lime juice, wine, and mustard for salad dressing. In large bowl, add the rest of the salad ingredients, topping with the avocado. Pour dressing over salad; cover; and refrigerate.

Preheat grill to medium high. Blend butter, chili oil, cayenne, and remaining lime juice. Brush butter mixture onto exposed crabmeat; place crab legs on grill; and cook 4 to 5 minutes, until heated. Save the unused sauce so that you can drizzle some over the crab legs at the table. Gently stir salad mixture to coat evenly; serve the dressed salad with the crab legs. ❋

TRINIDAD SALAD

½ cup extra-virgin olive oil
1 lime, juiced and divided
¼ cup dry white wine
2 tablespoons whole-grain mustard
1 can (14 to 15 ounces) palm hearts, drained and sliced crosswise
1 large, firm ripe papaya, skinned and chunked
1 cup thinly sliced celery
½ fresh small red chili pepper, sliced and minced
¼ small sweet onion, thinly sliced then quartered
2 large, firm ripe avocados, pitted and diced in large chunks

107 113 117

3 Steaks, Ribs & Burgers

CB's Grilled NY Strip Steak

- **2 8-ounce New York strip steaks, approximately 1 inch thick**
- **2 teaspoons kosher salt or sea salt**
- **1 teaspoon freshly ground black pepper**
- **2 tablespoons butter or oil**

Trim steaks of any excess fat and allow to rest, covered loosely with wax paper, for 15 minutes at room temperature.

Preheat a gas grill to high or until coals are white hot on a charcoal grill. Season steaks with salt and pepper; then brush steaks lightly on both sides with melted butter or oil.

Grill steaks for approximately 5 minutes. Turn once using a spatula, and cook for an additional 2 to 5 minutes, depending upon thickness.

Check for doneness using an instant-read thermometer (145°F for medium rare). Remove steaks to a warm platter, and allow to rest for at least 2 minutes before serving. ◎

Grilled Flank Steak with Lemon & Rosemary Marinade

1 flank steak, about 3 pounds
¼ cup olive oil
2 lemons, zested and juiced
2 tablespoons chopped fresh rosemary
2 cloves garlic, minced
1 teaspoon fresh ground black pepper
½ teaspoon coarse salt

Combine the marinade ingredients. Put the steak in a large plastic bag with the marinade, and seal. Turn several times to coat the steak. Refrigerate for 30 minutes to 4 hours.

Preheat one side of grill to high. Spray grates lightly with canola oil. Remove the steak from the marinade, and place directly on the high-heat side of the grill. Leave it alone until it develops a rich brown crust—3 to 5 minutes. Turn the steak, and repeat. Remove steak when it reaches 145°F for medium-rare. Cover loosely with foil, and let rest for 5 minutes. Carve into long slices at an angle, against the grain. ◎

Grilled Potato Planks, page 126

This recipe is courtesy of Brys Stephens at www.cookthink.com.

BBQ Chuck Steak

1½ pounds beef chuck, cut into ¾- to 1-inch-thick slices

MARINADE

1 cup finely chopped onion
1 cup ketchup
⅓ cup packed brown sugar
⅓ cup red wine vinegar
1 tablespoon Worcestershire sauce
⅛ teaspoon crushed red pepper

Combine marinade ingredients in a medium bowl. Place steak and 1 cup of marinade in food-safe plastic bag; turn to coat. Refrigerate remaining marinade.

Close bag securely. Marinate steak in refrigerator 6 hours or as long as overnight, turning occasionally. Remove steak; discard marinade. Place steak on the grill over medium heat. Grill, uncovered, 15 to 18 minutes for medium-rare to medium, turning occasionally.

Place refrigerated marinade in a small saucepan; bring to a boil. Reduce heat; simmer 10 to 15 minutes or until sauce thickens slightly, stirring occasionally.

Cut steak into serving-size pieces. Serve with sauce.

CB's Slow-Grilled Rib Eyes

2 rib-eye steaks, 8 to 12 ounces each, at least 1½ inches thick
Coarse salt
Canola, safflower, or peanut oil spray
2 teaspoons maître d' butter (See page 162.)

Trim away excess fat from around steaks. Blot moisture from meat using a paper towel. Generously sprinkle both sides of steaks with salt. Refrigerate for at least 1 hour.

Remove steaks from the refrigerator about 1 hour prior to grilling. Lightly brush off remaining salt.

Preheat one side of the grill to high, and leave the other side off. Spray steaks lightly with the oil, and place on the cool side of the grill, as far from the heat as you can.

When steaks reach an internal temperature of 90°F, use tongs to place them on the hot side of the grill. Sear steaks over direct heat until they reach a temperature of 140°F (rare) to 145°F (medium rare). Turn steaks once, when sear marks appear on each side. Remove from the grill, and top each steak with a teaspoon of maitre d' butter before serving. ◎

Here's a technique for grilling rib eyes that starts with low heat followed by an extremely hot finish for searing and crisping the meat.—CB

CB's Rib Eyes with Balsamic-Mushroom Sauce

2 rib-eye steaks, cut 1 to 2 inches thick
Coarse salt
Pepper
Canola oil spray

MUSHROOM SAUCE

8 ounces thinly sliced cremini or white mushrooms
¼ teaspoon salt
¾ cup balsamic vinegar
2 tablespoons butter
1 teaspoon crushed dried thyme leaves

Pat the steaks dry with a paper towel, and rub with salt. Refrigerate meat in a glass dish for 2 hours, removing it 30 minutes prior to grilling.

Trim ½ inch from the tip of each steak; mince and season with salt and pepper; and reserve.

Preheat grill to high; lightly spray steak with canola oil, and grill until the bottom edge begins to brown (about 3 minutes). Using tongs, turn over steaks and grill until that side of the meat begins to turn brown. Turn over the steaks again, and rotate them so that the grill grates are crossing the original sear marks. After 3 minutes, cross-hatch the other side. Finish steaks in an aluminum pan over indirect heat. Then let them rest at room temperature for 15 to 20 minutes.

Spray a sauté pan with canola oil, and place on the grill over medium heat. Brown the minced raw steak; then add the mushrooms and a pinch of salt. Sauté until mushrooms are tender.

Remove mushroom mixture, and set aside. Add balsamic vinegar to skillet; increase heat to medium high. Cook 7 to 10 minutes, stirring up any browned bits with a spatula. When the sauce is reduced to ¼ cup, stir in butter, thyme, cooked mushrooms, and a pinch of salt. Cook and stir until heated. Serve sauce with steaks. ◎

CB's Grilled Potatoes with Bacon, Cheese & Roasted Jalapenos, page 123

Montreal Grilled T-Bone

4 14-ounce T-bone steaks
½ cup beef stock
½ diced onion
½ teaspoon chili flakes
½ cup chicken broth
2 ounces bourbon
1 ounce port
¼ teaspoon Cajun seasoning
Salt and pepper to taste

Combine first six ingredients in medium sauce pan. Bring to a boil. Simmer uncovered for 4 minutes.

Sprinkle steaks with Cajun seasoning, salt, and pepper. Cook steaks on high heat until desired doneness. Place steaks on plate. Serve with sauce. ◎

2 Servings • Prep: 10 min. • Marinate: 45 min. • Grill: 8 min.

Flank-Steak Tournedos with Goat Cheese

4 2- to-3-ounce flank-steak slices, approximately 6 inches long and ½ inch or less thick
2 teaspoons coarse salt
2 teaspoons fresh ground black pepper
4 tablespoons extra-virgin olive oil
2 medium-size garlic cloves, minced
2 ounces goat cheese or other soft, creamy cheese
Butcher's twine

Flank steak is a flavorful cut that lends itself quite well to this recipe.

Place steak on cutting board or other hard surface, and cover with wax or parchment paper. Use mallet to flatten slightly.

Season meat with salt and pepper, and place in a shallow bowl. Cover with olive oil and minced garlic. Marinate for at least 45 minutes at room temperature. Lay the pieces of meat flat on a sheet of wax paper; spread softened goat cheese on each slice; roll up each one; and individually tie with string.

Preheat grill to high. Use tongs to place tournedos on grill, and allow them to sear for approximately 3 to 4 minutes. Turn meat; place on fresh section of grill; and sear for another 3 to 4 minutes.

Remove meat to a warming rack in a foil pan. Sprinkle additional crumbled goat cheese on tournedos, and allow to rest for a few minutes. Serve with cherry tomatoes, carrots, or other steamed vegetables. ◎

Happy "Holla" Brandy Pepper Steak

- **1 2-pound sirloin steak, 1½ to 2 inches thick**
- **2 teaspoons coarsely ground pepper**
- **½ cup beef bouillon**
- **1½ teaspoons salt**
- **½ cup Slivovitz (plum brandy) or regular brandy**
- **8 ounces mushrooms, cleaned and sliced (optional)**
- **1 teaspoon cornstarch**
- **2 tablespoons water**

Trim excess fat from steak and reserve. Render some of the fat in a large skillet that has been preheated on the grill over high heat.

Reduce heat to medium high. Sprinkle both sides of steak with pepper, and add to skillet. Cook until browned on each side. Reduce heat, and cook for 8 to 10 minutes. Remove steak to warm platter.

Drain pan drippings, reserving 2 teaspoons. Combine reserved drippings, bouillon, salt, and brandy in skillet. Add mushrooms, and cook until reduced by one-quarter, stirring constantly. Stir in cornstarch mixed with water. Cook until thickened, continuing to stir. Slice steak thinly across grain. Pour mixture over steak.

Ed Roith, of the Happy "Holla" Bar-B-Q team of Shawnee, Kansas, created this steak recipe, which is cooked in a skillet on top of the grill.

3–4 Servings • Prep: 15 min. • "Salt Cure": 4 hr.–overnight • Marinate: 2 hr. • Grill: 10–12 min. • Rest: 5 min.

CB's Salted Margarita Flank Steak

- **2 pounds flank or skirt steak**
- **Coarse salt**
- **3 shots tequila**
- **1 tablespoon Cointreau**
- **2 tablespoons lime zest**
- **2 tablespoons chopped fresh cilantro**
- **2 large garlic cloves, minced**
- **2 tablespoons hot sauce**

This dish benefits from an overnight "salt cure" to tenderize and flavor the meat.

Dry the meat with a paper towel. Liberally salt both sides of the steak; seal in plastic wrap; and place in refrigerator for at least 4 hours or overnight.

Mix together all remaining ingredients in a sealable plastic bag. Remove steak from plastic wrap; do not rinse off salt. Add steak to bag, and seal. Allow steak to marinate for up to 2 hours.

Preheat grill to high. Remove the steak from the marinade, and pat it dry. Spray the meat with canola oil. Cook until grill marks form, about 5 minutes. Use tongs to turn and sear the other side, about 5 minutes. Use an instant-read thermometer to check the temperature of the meat: 140°F rare, 145°F medium-rare, 160°F medium.

Transfer steak to a cutting board, and let rest for 5 minutes. Cut the steak across the grain at an angle to expose more of the pink meat—about ⅛- to ¼-inch-thick slices. Serve with your favorite salsa on the side. ◎

Ginger-Maple Steak with Napa Cabbage & Grilled Onions

- 2 boneless beef top-loin (strip) steaks, about 10 ounces each
- ¼ teaspoon black pepper
- 1 large red onion, cut into ½-inch-thick slices
- 4 cups thinly sliced Napa cabbage

GINGER-MAPLE MARINADE AND DRESSING

- ½ cup soy sauce
- ⅓ cup pure maple syrup
- ¼ cup lemon juice
- 2 tablespoons minced fresh ginger
- 1 tablespoon sesame oil
- 1½ teaspoons minced fresh garlic
- 1½ teaspoons Asian chile-garlic paste

Whisk marinade ingredients in a medium bowl. Place steaks and ½ cup marinade in a plastic bag; turn steaks to coat. Seal bag, and refrigerate up to 2 hours. Cover and refrigerate remaining marinade for dressing.

Preheat grill to medium high. Remove steaks from marinade; discard marinade. Sprinkle steaks with pepper. Place steaks in center of grill; arrange onion around steaks. Grill steaks, uncovered, 15 to 18 minutes for medium-rare to medium, turning occasionally. Grill onions 15 to 20 minutes, turning occasionally.

Carve steaks into slices. Cut onion into quarters. Toss cabbage, onion, and 2 tablespoons reserved dressing in a large bowl. Arrange beef on cabbage mixture. Drizzle with the remaining dressing. ◎

4 Servings • Prep: 5 min. • Marinate: 8 hr. • Grill: 18 min. • Rest: 5 min.

CB's Grilled Hanger Steak "Moutarde"

12-to-18-ounce hanger or flank steak
½ cup grainy Dijon mustard
2 tablespoons maple syrup
1 tablespoon cider vinegar
¼ teaspoon dried tarragon
¼ teaspoon hot sauce
Salt and pepper to taste
Canola oil spray

Combine the first 7 ingredients in a plastic bag; massage gently to coat. Marinate in refrigerator for up to 8 hours.

Preheat grill to high. Remove steak from bag; spray with canola oil; and grill on each side for about 4 minutes. Remove; place in an aluminum pan; and cover with foil. Place on warming shelf over indirect heat, and continue cooking for about 10 minutes. Remove from grill, and let steak rest, covered, for about 5 minutes. Slice into thin strips across the grain. ◎

Several years ago, I had the opportunity to visit the Burgundy region of France, where I was delighted to see a grilled steak with "frites"(fries) on the menu at just about every restaurant! Here's my interpretation of those steaks.—CB

Grilled Tenderloins with Blue Cheese Topping

2 tenderloin steaks, approximately ½ pound each
1 large clove garlic, halved
½ teaspoon salt
½ teaspoon chopped fresh parsley

Combine topping ingredients in a small bowl. Rub steaks with garlic halves.

Place steaks on hot grill, and cook 8 to 11 minutes, turning occasionally. One to two minutes before steaks are done, season with salt; then top evenly with cheese mixture. Remove from grill; sprinkle with parsley; and serve.

TOPPING

2 tablespoons cream cheese
4 teaspoons crumbled blue cheese
4 teaspoons plain yogurt
2 teaspoons minced onion
Dash ground white pepper

6–8 Servings • Prep: 15 min. • Rest: 1 hr. • Grill: 15–20 min. • Rest after cooking: 15–20 min.

CB's Hawaiian-Style Tri-Tip

2½ pounds tri-tip roast (triangular tip of the sirloin)
Pineapple slices
Vegetable oil spray

DRY RUB

2 tablespoons coarse salt
½ tablespoon cracked black pepper
1 tablespoon minced garlic

GLAZE

1 tablespoon brown sugar
2 tablespoons butter, melted
1 tablespoon light soy sauce
1 tablespoon finely grated fresh ginger

Combine dry-rub ingredients; apply to all surfaces of the meat; wrap meat in plastic; and allow meat to rest at room temperature for 1 hour.

Preheat one side of grill to high. Remove meat from plastic, and lightly spray with vegetable oil on all sides. Place on hot side of grill to sear for about 2 to 3 minutes on each side, using tongs to turn.

Thoroughly combine glaze ingredients in a small bowl. Place seared roast in pan on cool half of grill; apply glaze with silicon brush; and close hood. Cook until internal temperature of meat reaches 145°F for medium rare, 160°F for medium. (Tri-tip is best enjoyed medium rare.) Transfer roast to carving board; tent with foil; and let stand for 15 to 20 minutes. Grill pineapple slices 2 to 3 minutes on each side. ◎

The glaze for this steak reminds me of the flavors of Hawaii, where one of my favorite meals is the "Plate Lunch." It usually features either chicken, fish, beef, or pork prepared with fresh ginger, garlic, and soy sauce.—CB

CB's Tailgate Cheese Steaks

2 onions, thinly sliced
1 pound sirloin steak (you can also use lamb, pork, or chicken)
Salt and pepper
4 cups shredded cheddar, jack, or havarti cheese
4 hoagie rolls
4 sheets heavy-duty foil

Preheat grill to medium high. Spray foil with nonstick cooking spray, and place one-quarter of the onion slices on each sheet.

Cut meat into strips ⅛ inch thick; season with salt and pepper. Add one-quarter of the steak strips, followed by one-quarter of the cheese to the onions on each foil sheet. Fold foil over mixture, sealing edges firmly. Leave some space for food to expand during cooking.

Grill 10 minutes on covered grill, turning once. Serve on hoagie rolls, topped with favorite BBQ sauce. ◎

This is a great preparation method for picnics, tailgating, or any time you have a large group of folks to serve. Prepare the foil packets in advance, keep cool, and place on the grill as you need them.—CB

10 Servings • Prep: 20 min. • Marinate: 24–30 hr. • Grill: 15 min.

Pomsey's Tailgate Tips

9 pounds sirloin tips or rib-eye cubes
French rolls
American cheese
Vidalia onion, grilled

SAUCE

1 cup ketchup
⅛ tablespoon molasses
⅓ teaspoon spicy brown or Dijon mustard
⅙ teaspoon soy sauce
⅓ teaspoon garlic powder
⅓ teaspoon hot pepper sauce
1 teaspoon black pepper

Trim any excess fat (keeping in mind the meat needs some fat to remain juicy throughout the grilling process), and cut meat into 2-inch cubes. Place tips in a large plastic container or bag.

In a large mixing bowl, combine sauce ingredients. Set aside some sauce for basting if you desire, and pour the rest of the sauce over tips. Mix well so that meat is completely coated. Refrigerate for 24 to 30 hours.

Preheat grill to medium-high heat. Grill tips to your desired doneness. Serve on rolls with cheese and onions. Note: to avoid a messy grill, coat your tips well the day before so that there's no need to slather on extra sauce. ◎

"Sizzle on the Grill" contributor Greg from Quincy, Massachusetts, writes that his gang enjoys these tips on fresh French rolls with American cheese and grilled Vidalia onions. This recipe feeds 10 if other main courses are served.

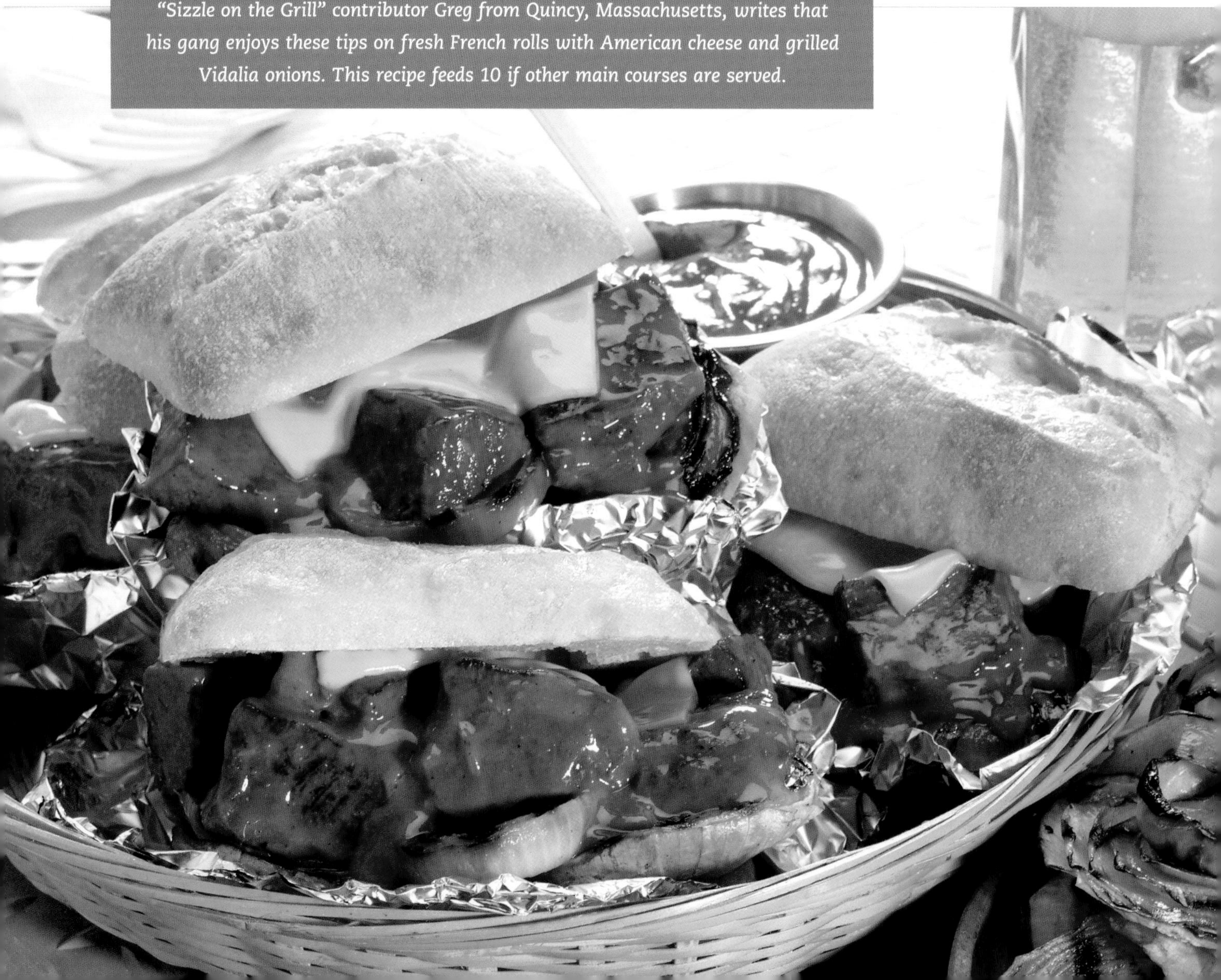

Bloody Mary London Broil

1 London broil (3½ pounds)
2 cups tomato juice
¼ cup Worcestershire sauce
3 tablespoons prepared horseradish
3 tablespoons dry sherry
2 teaspoons crushed dried marjoram
1 teaspoon crushed dried basil
1 teaspoon freshly ground black pepper

Combine tomato juice, Worcestershire sauce, horseradish, sherry, and seasonings in a bowl. Spread the steak out in a single layer in a baking dish. Spoon tomato-juice mixture over meat, spreading to cover. Turn meat to coat other side. Cover and refrigerate for at least 2 hours, or set aside at room temperature for 30 minutes.

Remove meat from marinade, and discard marinade. Grill steak over medium-high heat for 8 minutes. Turn and grill for 7 to 10 minutes longer for medium rare, or until desired doneness.

Let steak rest at room temperature for approximately 5 minutes. Slice steak diagonally into thin strips before serving. ◎

2 Servings • Prep: 30 min. • Marinate: 2 hr.–overnight • Grill: 40 min.

Porterhouse with Spicy Parmesan Butter

1 Porterhouse steak, approximately 3 inches thick
¼ cup olive oil
8 garlic cloves, minced
1 tablespoon chopped fresh thyme
1 tablespoon salt
2 teaspoons ground black pepper
1½ teaspoons chopped fresh rosemary
Spicy Parmesan Butter (See recipe, below.)

Prepare butter by mixing all ingredients in a small bowl until blended. (Can be made 2 days ahead.) Refrigerate. When ready to use, remove from refrigerator and warm to room temperature.

Place steak in a glass dish. Whisk oil and next five ingredients in a small bowl to blend. Pour half of marinade over steak. Turn steak over, and coat with remaining marinade. Cover and refrigerate at least 2 hours and up to 24 hours, turning steak occasionally.

Preheat grill to medium. Remove meat from marinade, and grill to desired doneness or until internal temperature reaches 115°F to 130°F for medium-rare, approximately 18 minutes per side. Transfer steak to a platter; cover; and let rest for 5 minutes.

Cutting away from bone, slice each meat section into ⅓-inch slices. Spread Spicy Parmesan Butter over each portion, and serve. ◎

SPICY PARMESAN BUTTER

3 tablespoons butter, room temperature
2 teaspoons grated Parmesan cheese
1 anchovy fillet, drained and minced
1 teaspoon paprika
½ teaspoon Dijon mustard
½ teaspoon Worcestershire sauce
¼ teaspoon ground black pepper
¼ teaspoon Tabasco sauce

CB's Chili-Rubbed Ribs

4 pounds of pork ribs, trimmed of excess fat

CHILI RUB

2 tablespoons chili powder
2 tablespoons garlic powder
1 tablespoon ground ginger
1 tablespoon smoked paprika
1 tablespoon ground cumin
1 teaspoon salt
1 teaspoon ground black pepper

Whisk chili-rub ingredients together in small bowl to blend. After drying ribs with a paper towel, rub spice mixture all over ribs. (Use food-safe gloves.) Wrap ribs in plastic wrap, and refrigerate for at least 6 hours or overnight.

SAUCE

6 ounces dark beer
18 ounces barbecue sauce
1 cup water
2 tablespoons honey
1 tablespoon instant espresso powder

Combine in saucepan, and simmer until sauce thickens. Cool slightly; then cover and refrigerate until needed.

Preheat grill, and set up for indirect heat to 200°F to 225°F (low). Add wood chips, if desired. Remove ribs from refrigerator, and unwrap. Place them on indirect heat side of the grill, bone-side down. Pour some of the sauce into a pan, and place over indirect heat. Close hood, and slow cook, monitoring temperature regularly. After 1 hour, brush ribs with sauce. Close hood, and allow ribs to cook 1 hour more, checking at 20-minute intervals and applying more sauce.

Ribs should be fully cooked after 2 hours. To keep warm on the grill for up to 1 hour, wrap ribs in 2 layers of heavy-duty aluminum foil (shiny side out) that has been sprayed on the dull side with canola oil. Add the remainder of the sauce before sealing. ◎

Beer-Basted Baby Back Ribs

8 pounds baby back pork ribs, cut into 4-rib sections
6 cups beer
2½ cups brown sugar
1½ cups apple cider vinegar
1½ tablespoons chili powder
1½ tablespoons ground cumin
1 tablespoon dry mustard
2 teaspoons salt
2 teaspoons dried crushed red pepper
2 bay leaves

Bring first nine ingredients to a boil in a large pot. Reduce heat, and simmer about 1 minute to blend flavors. Add half of ribs to sauce. Cover pot, and simmer until ribs are tender, turning frequently, about 25 minutes. Transfer ribs to baking dish. Repeat with remaining ribs. Boil barbecue sauce until reduced to 3 cups, about 40 minutes. Discard bay leaves. (Can be prepared 1 day ahead. Cover ribs and sauce separately, and refrigerate. Warm sauce before continuing.)

Preheat grill to medium, and oil the grill grates. Brush ribs with some of sauce; sprinkle with salt. Grill ribs until heated through, browned, and well-glazed, brushing occasionally with sauce, about 6 minutes per side. ◎

CB's Texas-Style Beef Ribs

2 racks of beef back ribs (7 ribs per rack)
2 tablespoons black pepper
1 tablespoon smoked paprika
1 tablespoon ground mustard
½ teaspoon ground cayenne pepper

Combine all spices. Rub over surface of ribs to coat well. Wrap with plastic, and chill for up to 4 hours.

Set grill for indirect cooking, and preheat to medium high with hood closed. Place ribs on rack in roasting pan. Add ½-inch of water to bottom of pan. Tent pan with foil, but leave sides open to allow smoke to enter. Place wood chips in smoker box or on grate. Cook ribs for about 2 hours. Remove ribs from pan, and place on grill over medium heat for 15 minutes. Cut between ribs to serve. ◎

Peg's Magic Beans, page 120

When I lived in Texas, I learned that a Texan's concept of barbecue is an appreciation of the meat—the flavors that evolve after careful preparation and attention to spices, heat, and smoke. So serve these ribs with sauce if you dare!—CB

Pork Spareribs with Coconut-Peanut Sauce

3 to 4 pounds pork spareribs

COCONUT-PEANUT SAUCE

⅓ cup light coconut milk
¼ cup creamy peanut butter
2 tablespoons soy sauce
1 tablespoon sesame oil
1 tablespoon minced ginger
1 tablespoon snipped cilantro
¼ to ½ teaspoon crushed red pepper, or to taste
1 garlic clove, minced

Why make the same old barbecued ribs? Try this sauce for your next cookout. Serve with tropical fruit salad and rice.

Grill ribs over indirect medium heat for 1 hour. Stir together sauce ingredients until well combined; reserve half of sauce to serve with finished ribs. Brush remaining sauce on ribs; grill for 30 minutes longer until ribs are tender and meat pulls from the bone. Warm reserved sauce, and serve with ribs. ◎

Cola Ribs

2 racks baby back ribs, approx. 3 pounds each
3 sweet potatoes
3 ears corn
Canola oil

MARINADE

2 cups cola
½ cup bourbon
½ cup brown sugar
2 tablespoons mustard powder
2 tablespoons chili flakes
1 tablespoon minced garlic
3 sprigs fresh rosemary
½ bag char wood (⅔ soaked in cool water for 2 hours or until saturated)

Place ribs in nonreactive glass dish. Mix marinade ingredients in medium-size bowl. Pour marinade over ribs, and cover with plastic wrap. Allow ribs to marinate for 4 hours.

Preheat grill to medium heat for indirect cooking. Add two-thirds of drained soaked wood and remaining dry char wood to smoking tray. Mix, and allow wood to smoke. Once smoke is achieved, reduce heat to low, and add more wet chips.

Place ribs over the side of the grill that does not have direct heat. Close lid, and smoke for 3 hours or until ribs are falling off the bone. While cooking, continue to add wet chips to the tray. Remove ribs from grill, and loosely tent them with foil. Let ribs rest for 10 minutes before serving.

Spray potatoes with canola oil. Sear potatoes 3 minutes on each side. Move to tray over indirect heat, and cook for 20 minutes or until tender; grill corn over direct heat, turning often, for about 5 minutes. ◎

Asian-Style Baby Back Ribs

2 racks baby backs or other favorite ribs

Stir all barbecue sauce ingredients together.

Coat ribs evenly on both sides with one-half of the sauce. Reserve remaining sauce to serve with ribs. Marinate ribs, refrigerated, for at least 1 hour. For more flavor, marinate overnight.

Preheat grill to medium (325°F), and oil grill grates. Baste ribs occasionally with marinade during cooking, stopping 15 minutes before removing ribs from grill.

To serve, cut each side of ribs in half, or into individual ribs. Serve immediately with remaining sauce. ◎

ASIAN BARBECUE SAUCE

(makes 3 cups)
6 cloves garlic, minced
2 tablespoons finely minced ginger
8 serrano peppers, minced, including seeds
4 small green onions, green and white parts, minced
¼ cup minced cilantro
1 tablespoon grated lime zest
Juice from 3 limes
1 cup hoisin sauce
½ cup wine vinegar
¼ cup Thai fish sauce
¼ cup honey
2 tablespoons soy sauce
2 tablespoons canola oil

Indian Tandoori Ribs

2 slabs pork spareribs

MARINADE

2 8-ounce cartons plain yogurt
2 garlic cloves, crushed
3 tablespoons grated ginger root
2 jalapeño chilies, seeded
½ cup fresh cilantro leaves
1 tablespoon ground cumin
Red food coloring

Tandoori refers to the Indian traditional red-orange tint of tandoor-oven cooking. Serve with flatbread or naan, seasoned rice mixed with peas, and cucumber salad.

In a blender, combine yogurt, garlic, ginger, chilies, cilantro, and cumin, and puree. Reserve a small amount for use as dipping sauce if desired. Add a few drops of red food coloring. Place ribs in large plastic bag; coat with marinade; seal bag; and refrigerate overnight.

Preheat grill to medium. Drain ribs, and discard marinade. Place ribs over drip pan; close grill hood; and cook for 1½ hours over indirect heat, until ribs are tender. ◎

Tomato-Basil Ribs with Zesty Ranch Dressing

6 boneless country-style pork ribs
½ cup margarine, softened
1 medium tomato, halved and thinly sliced
1 1-ounce package basil leaves
¼ teaspoon salt or to taste
⅛ teaspoon black pepper or to taste
1 cup ranch-style dressing
½ teaspoon hot pepper sauce
Butcher's twine

Lance Hensley of Montgomery, Alabama, created this first-place recipe for stuffed, country-style ribs for the Alabama National Fair.

Preheat grill to medium high. Slice each rib down center lengthwise, cutting halfway through. Spread equal amounts of margarine down center of each rib. Arrange tomato slices and basil leaves down center of each. Wrap each rib with butcher's twine in several places to hold rib together. Sprinkle evenly with salt and pepper.

Grill ribs 15 to 18 minutes or until no longer pink in center, turning frequently using spatula or tongs to handle easily. Watch closely for flare-ups. Margarine will melt and flames will occur. Move pieces to another area of grill when this happens. Combine salad dressing and hot pepper sauce in small bowl, and stir until well blended. Serve as dip for ribs. ◎

CB's Tailgate Grilled Baby Back Ribs

1-pound rack of baby back ribs per person
Coarse salt and fresh ground pepper to taste
¼ cup brown sugar per rack of ribs
¼ cup apple cider vinegar per rack
¼ cup your favorite barbecue sauce per rack

This is an easy recipe to prepare at home and finish at a tailgate party.

Have the butcher remove the thin membrane from the back of the ribs. Rinse the ribs, and pat dry. Rub each rack thoroughly with salt and pepper and then the ½ cup of brown sugar. Note: it's a good idea to use food-safe gloves during this process.

Place the ribs, meat side down, in a nonreactive bowl or pan, and pour cider vinegar over them. Cover ribs with plastic wrap and refrigerate. Marinate for a minimum of 2 hours. Remove the ribs from the refrigerator, and discard the marinade.

Preheat one side of the grill to medium high; reserve the other side for indirect cooking. You can add wood chips for smoke flavor for the first hour.

Place the ribs on the hot side, and sear for about 5 minutes. Then use tongs to transfer to the side without direct heat. Close hood; reduce heat to low; and roast for about 2 hours. Maintain an even temperature of about 225°F to 250°F.

NOTE: you can also finish the ribs in the oven. Just place them on a baking sheet in an oven set to about 225°F to 250°F for about 1½ hours to 2 hours. Use tongs to grab each rack. If the rib rack bends and starts to separate, ribs are ready!

TO TRANSPORT: Up to 1 hour in advance, baste ribs with barbecue sauce, and seal in aluminum foil. Place in insulated carrier. Once on site, you can place one or two of the foil packages on the grill, heated to low, and close the lid to warm the ribs. When the ribs have warmed, remove them from foil, and turn grill to medium high. Sear ribs on direct heat, brushing on remaining sauce, if needed. To serve, slice individual ribs, and pile on platter with more sauce if desired. ◎

CB's Nut-Crusted Ribs with Bourbon Mop Sauce

2 whole racks (about 4 to 5 pounds) pork spareribs
½ cup apple cider vinegar
½ cup dark porter beer, or stout
3 to 4 cups finely chopped pecans, walnuts, or almonds

DRY RUB

1 tablespoon garlic powder
1 tablespoon chili powder
1 tablespoon onion powder
1 tablespoon mustard powder
1 tablespoon cumin
1 teaspoon kosher salt
1 teaspoon freshly ground black pepper
1 cup dark brown sugar

BOURBON MOP SAUCE

¼ pound butter
1 cup dark brown sugar
4 cups ketchup
½ cup apple cider vinegar
6 garlic cloves, crushed and finely minced
2 teaspoon curry powder
Contents of 1 Earl Grey tea bag
1 tablespoon stone-ground mustard
4 ounces Worcestershire sauce
1 ounce Tabasco sauce
2 cups Kentucky bourbon

Combine and briefly simmer the mop-sauce ingredients, except the bourbon; add the bourbon; then remove from heat. Refrigerate, covered, for at least 2 days. The night before cooking, remove the cover and air dry the ribs in the refrigerator for 1 hour. Then coat them with a mixture of vinegar and beer; massage them with the dry rub; wrap tightly in plastic; and refrigerate overnight.

Preheat grill and prepare a smoker box using the chips of your choice. Smoke ribs for 2½ hours in low (225°F), indirect heat. Then place them on heavy aluminum foil; coat with warmed mop sauce and the nuts; wrap; and cook for at least 1 hour with the grill lid closed. When meat easily pulls away from the bone, place the ribs on the grates to finish, adding more sauce and nuts. ◎

Kansas City Mop Ribs

6 to 8 pounds pork spare ribs, long ends only

KANSAS CITY DRY RUB (makes ⅔ cup)

2 tablespoons brown sugar
2 tablespoons ground paprika
1 tablespoon white sugar
1 tablespoon garlic salt
1 tablespoon celery salt
1 tablespoon chili powder
2 teaspoons freshly ground black pepper
1 teaspoon ground cayenne chili
½ teaspoon dry mustard

Combine all ingredients in a bowl, and mix well. Store any unused rub in sealed container in freezer.

KANSAS CITY-STYLE BARBECUE SAUCE (makes 1½ cups)

1 small onion, chopped
2 cloves garlic, minced
1 tablespoon vegetable oil
1 cup ketchup
⅓ cup molasses
¼ cup distilled white vinegar
2 tablespoons chili powder
2 teaspoons dry mustard
1 teaspoon celery salt
1 teaspoon paprika
1 teaspoon ground cayenne chili
½ teaspoon freshly ground black pepper
¼ cup water or more if needed

Sauté onion and garlic in oil until onion is soft. Add remaining ingredients; simmer for 30 minutes or until thickened.

Sprinkle rub evenly over ribs, and let marinate for 2 hours at room temperature or overnight in refrigerator. Prepare smoker, and place ribs on grates. Smoke at approximately 200°F for 4 hours. Baste frequently with sauce during last 30 minutes of smoking. Serve with additional sauce on the side. ◎

Montreal Jerk Ribs

2 racks baby back ribs

Rub dry ingredients onto all surfaces of ribs. Grill ribs over indirect heat about 1½ hours in covered grill, turning occasionally, until ribs are very tender. (Or roast ribs on rack in shallow pan in a 350°F oven for 1½ hours.) Cut into one- or two-rib portions to serve. ◎

MONTREAL JERK RUB

2 tablespoons minced dried onions
1 tablespoon onion powder
4 teaspoons ground thyme
2 teaspoons salt
2 teaspoons ground allspice
½ teaspoon ground nutmeg
½ teaspoon ground cinnamon
1 tablespoon sugar
2 teaspoons black pepper
1 teaspoon cayenne

In a small jar with a tight-fitting lid, shake together all dry ingredients until blended.

Hickory Beef Ribs

2 racks beef ribs, 8–10 ribs each

RIB MIXTURE

½ cup soy sauce
1 tablespoon steak spice
1 tablespoon garlic salt
1 tablespoon chopped fresh garlic
1 teaspoon chili flakes

SAUCE

1 large onion, diced
1 tablespoon olive oil
3 28-ounce cans tomato sauce
1 19-ounce jar applesauce
2 cups brown sugar
1 cup honey
½ cup soy sauce
½ cup white vinegar
4 tablespoons molasses
1¼ teaspoons liquid smoke
Salt and pepper

Fill a large pot with water, and add rib mixture. Bring water to a boil. Add ribs; boil for 1 hour.

Sauté diced onion in olive oil until soft. Add remaining ingredients to a large sauce pot; bring to a boil; then continue to simmer over medium heat for 30 minutes. Remove ribs from water, and pat dry with paper towels. Coat with enough sauce to cover; let stand 30 minutes. Grill ribs on medium high for 8 to 10 minutes, basting and turning often to avoid burning. ◎

Mustard-Bourbon Baby Back Ribs

3 racks baby back ribs (4 to 6 pounds)

SPICE RUB

2 tablespoons ground cumin
1 tablespoon chili powder
1 tablespoon dry mustard
1 tablespoon coarse salt
1½ teaspoons cayenne pepper
1½ teaspoons ground cardamom
1½ teaspoons ground cinnamon

Mix ingredients in medium bowl.

Rub spice mixture over both sides of rib racks. Arrange ribs on a large baking sheet. Cover, and refrigerate overnight. Preheat grill to medium, and oil grill grates. Cut rib racks into four to six rib sections, and arrange on cooking grate. Grill until meat is tender, turning occasionally, for about 40 minutes. Cut sections between bones into individual ribs, and lay flat in baking dish. Transfer 3 cups sauce to small bowl; place remaining sauce in small saucepan; and reserve. Brush ribs with sauce from bowl. Return ribs to grill. Place pan of reserved sauce at edge of grill to warm. Grill ribs until brown and crisp on edges, brushing with more sauce from bowl and turning occasionally, about 10 minutes.

Serve ribs with warm sauce. ◎

SAUCE

1 tablespoon vegetable oil
2 bunches scallions, chopped
2 cups chopped white onions
8 garlic cloves, chopped
2 cups brown sugar
1 cup ketchup
1 cup tomato paste
1 cup Dijon mustard
1 cup water
½ cup Worcestershire sauce
½ cup apple cider vinegar
½ cup apple juice
1 large dried ancho chili, stemmed, seeded, and cut into small pieces
1 tablespoon ground cumin
1½ cups bourbon
Salt and pepper, to taste

Heat oil in large pot over medium-low heat. Add scallions, onions, and garlic; sauté until tender. Mix in remaining ingredients, adding bourbon last. Simmer sauce, stirring occasionally, until reduced to 7 cups, about 1 hour. Season to taste with salt and pepper. Refrigerate in covered container for up to 2 weeks.

CB's Burgers with Caramelized Onion Spread

1 pound 80-percent-lean ground chuck
1 tablespoon garlic powder
1 teaspoon cumin powder
1 teaspoon coarse salt or to taste
1 teaspoon freshly ground black pepper or to taste
Chopped or shredded spinach leaves
1 medium tomato
2 sesame-seed burger buns, buttered

CARAMELIZED ONION SPREAD

1 large yellow onion
Canola oil spray
¼ cup ketchup
1 tablespoon dry mustard
2 tablespoons sour cream
1 teaspoon balsamic vinegar
1 teaspoon brown sugar or honey

Combine ground beef, garlic, cumin, salt, and pepper in a large mixing bowl. Gently form into two patties about ½ to 1 inch thick. Place in refrigerator for at least 1 hour prior to grilling.

While patties are chilling, heat grill to medium high. Slice onion into ½-inch disks; separate into rings; and spray with canola oil. Use tongs to place on the grill. When the onions are caramelized and soft, place them into a food processor or blender. Add ketchup, mustard, sour cream, balsamic vinegar, and brown sugar. Pulse until mixture is thick and chunky. Cover with foil, and place on warming rack while burgers cook.

Remove patties from refrigerator, and lightly spray with canola oil before placing them on the grill over medium-high heat. Cook for about 4 to 5 minutes per side, turning once with a spatula that has been sprayed with canola oil. Place patties in a foil pan on cooler section of the grill to continue cooking over indirect heat. Cook until meat reaches an internal temperature of 160°F.

While the patties are finishing, butter the buns, and toast on the grill. Add each burger to a bottom bun, and spread with spoonfuls of the caramelized onion mixture. Top with sliced tomatoes, spinach leaves, and then with the top bun. ◎

Holy Guacamole Burgers

2 pounds ground chuck
2 to 3 heads of garlic, roasted
2 cups mayonnaise
½ teaspoon lemon juice
1 tablespoon Worcestershire sauce
1 teaspoon coarse salt
½ teaspoon freshly ground black pepper
2 tablespoons Tex-Mex Rub (See below.)
6 thick slices ripe tomato
6 lettuce leaves
6 large hamburger buns
Pre-made guacamole
Salt and freshly ground pepper to taste

Mix all ingredients for the Tex-Mex Rub in a small bowl. Set aside.

For garlic mayonnaise, squeeze one bulb roasted garlic from its skin into a medium bowl. Using fork, mash garlic, pressing against side of bowl. Add mayonnaise and lemon juice, and mix well. Refrigerate mixture until ready to serve burgers.

Place second bulb of roasted garlic in a large bowl, and mash with fork against side of bowl. Add ground chuck, Worcestershire sauce, salt, and pepper, and mix with hands until just combined. Gently form six patties approximately ½ to ¾ inches thick. Coat patties with dry rub.

Preheat grill to high. Grill burgers for approximately 1 minute on each side. Reduce grill temperature to medium, and continue cooking burgers for 4 to 5 minutes more per side. Toast buns at edge of grill. Spread garlic mayonnaise on one half of each bun, and top with lettuce, burger, guacamole, and tomato slice. Sprinkle with salt and pepper. ◎

TEX-MEX RUB

2 tablespoons chili powder
4 teaspoons garlic salt
2½ teaspoons onion powder
2 teaspoons ground cumin
1½ teaspoons dried oregano
¾ teaspoon cayenne pepper

Tomato-Mozzarella-Polenta Burgers

1½ pounds ground beef
⅔ cup balsamic vinegar
Salt and pepper
1 package (16 to 18 ounces) refrigerated polenta, cut into 8 disks
2 tablespoons olive oil
1 package (8 ounces) fresh mozzarella cheese, cut into 8 slices
2 medium tomatoes cut into 4 slices each
Fresh basil, thinly sliced

Bring vinegar to a boil in a 2-quart saucepan. Reduce heat; simmer uncovered for 9 to 10 minutes or until reduced to ⅓ cup. Set aside.

Preheat grill to medium high. Lightly shape ground beef into eight ½-inch-thick patties. Season burgers with salt and pepper. Brush polenta slices with oil.

Place patties in center of grill; arrange polenta disks around patties. Grill patties for 4 to 5 minutes per side, turning once and basting with 2 tablespoons reduced vinegar after turning. About 2 minutes before burgers are done, top each with a slice of mozzarella to warm and soften, taking care not to let cheese melt onto grill. Cook until centers of burgers reach 160°F. Cook polenta, turning once, until heated through and light grill marks appear on each side, about 9 to 10 minutes. For each serving, place burger on top of polenta and tomato slice. Drizzle with remaining vinegar, and sprinkle with basil to garnish. ◎

CB's Inside-Out & Upside-Down Burgers

1 pound lean ground beef
6 strips lean bacon, cooked but not crisp, chopped
1 cup shredded cheese mix, such as cheddar and jack cheese
3 tablespoons olive oil
½ teaspoon Worcestershire sauce
1 clove garlic, minced
4 tablespoons unsalted butter
2 teaspoons sea salt or kosher salt
Freshly ground black pepper
3 hamburger buns

In a large mixing bowl, gently fold together ground beef, bacon, cheese, olive oil, Worcestershire sauce, and garlic. Form mixture into three round balls. Gently press burger balls into 1- to 2-inch-thick patties. Chill for at least 30 minutes.

Preheat the grill to high. Melt butter in a small saucepan. Remove burgers from the refrigerator; season with salt and pepper to taste.

Lightly brush one side of each burger with melted butter; place, buttered side down, on one side of grill; and reduce heat on that side to medium, leaving other side of grill on high. Cook for approximately 7 minutes with lid closed.

Open lid, and brush top of burgers with remaining butter. Using an oiled spatula, gently lift patties; place, buttered side down, on opposite side of grill over high heat. Reduce heat on that side to medium and close lid. Cook for 5 minutes. Let patties rest, covered with foil, for approximately 2 minutes. Place on buns, and serve. ◎

Beer Burgers Smashed with Fresh Goat Cheese

1½ pounds ground beef
1 teaspoon salt
2 tablespoons onion, minced
6 slices goat cheese, chilled until firm
⅓ can beer
3 tablespoons steak sauce
⅓ cup ketchup
1 tablespoon prepared mustard
1 tablespoon sugar
6 hamburger or potato buns, buttered

Combine first three ingredients, and shape meat into half patties. Place slice of goat cheese on one half; then put another half patty on top to form whole burger.

Combine next five ingredients, and heat in a saucepan until mixture thickens. Keep warm.

Preheat grill to high. Place patties in an oiled grill basket; grill 4 to 6 minutes on each side. Toast hamburger buns on edge of grill, turning once, for approximately 2 minutes. Place patties in buns, and top with warm sauce before serving. ◎

Cajun Burgers

- **2 pounds ground beef**
- **1 cup seasoned breadcrumbs**
- **2 tablespoons ground coriander**
- **2 tablespoons Cajun spice**
- **¼ teaspoon dried steak seasoning**
- **¼ teaspoon dried oregano**
- **1 teaspoon Worcestershire sauce**
- **¼ teaspoon garlic powder**
- **2 jalapeño peppers, seeded and diced**
- **6 to 8 hamburger buns, toasted**

Combine all ingredients except the buns in a large mixing bowl with ground beef. Form into patties, 6–8 ounces each.

Cook on high heat until desired doneness, 6 to 8 minutes per side for medium. ◎

Thai-Style Burgers

1 pound coarse-ground 80-percent-lean beef
1 large shallot, finely chopped
2 green onions, coarsely chopped, including greens
4 to 7 garlic cloves, finely chopped
1 roasted poblano pepper, finely chopped (or use paste)
1 roasted habanero pepper, finely chopped (or use paste)
2 to 3 tablespoons freshly grated ginger
2 to 3 tablespoons Thai green curry paste, plus additional for topping
Cayenne pepper to taste (optional)
Coarse salt
Black pepper
Breadcrumbs (optional)
Canola oil spray
½ lime
Grated lime zest
3 to 4 buns, toasted
½ bunch fresh cilantro or watercress sprigs
Bean sprouts
Basil

In large nonreactive bowl, thoroughly mix the 10 ingredients that follow the ground beef. Gently fold mixture into the meat, being careful not to overwork. If the meat is too loose, add bread crumbs until you can form 3 or 4 patties about 1 inch thick. Chill for at least 1 hour.

Preheat grill to medium high. Remove burgers from refrigerator, and lightly spray with canola oil before placing them on the grill. When you see some browning at the edges (about 2 to 3 minutes), spray a spatula with canola oil. Slip the spatula under the burger patty; away from the heat, spray the uncooked side; and then place it down on a clean section of grate. Grill over direct heat for another 2 to 3 minutes or until the meat is seared. Use the same method to lift patties and place them in a holding pan over indirect heat. Cook until internal temperature of patties reaches 160°F.

Before serving the burgers on toasted buns, squeeze a few drops of lime juice onto each one, along with some grated lime zest. Serve with cilantro or watercress and bean sprouts topped with a dollop of green curry paste if desired. ◎

121

127

137

141

4 Sides

7–10 Servings • Prep: 20 min. + overnight refrigeration • Cook: 4–5 hr.

Peg's Magic Beans

1 pound maple-cured bacon
1 large white onion, finely chopped
1 pound 80-percent-lean ground beef
1 can (15½ ounces) dark-red kidney beans
1 can (15½ ounces) white cannellini beans or great northern beans
1 can (15½ ounces) black-eyed peas or navy beans
1 can (8 ounces) baked beans
1 can (15½ ounces) medium to hot chili beans
1 bottle (12 ounces) chili sauce
1 cup brown sugar
6 ounces apple cider vinegar
1 tablespoon garlic powder
1 tablespoon chili powder
½ tablespoon paprika
Hot sauce to taste

The night before cooking beans, fry one pound of maple-cured bacon in a large skillet or frying pan until crisp. Remove the bacon; crumble when cool. Drain fat from skillet, reserving about 1 teaspoon. Cook onion and ground beef in the skillet with the reserved bacon fat until meat is browned. Drain off the fat, and transfer the onion, cooked ground beef, and bacon to the cooking sleeve of a 5-quart slow cooker.

Drain and rinse all of the beans except the chili and baked beans. Then add all of the beans, chili sauce, brown sugar, vinegar, and spices to the rest of the ingredients. Stir well. Cover with plastic wrap, and store in the refrigerator overnight.

The next day, transfer the cooking sleeve with the beans and meat to the slow cooker set on low for a minimum of 4 cooking hours. Serve warm. ❖

From "Sizzle on the Grill." I can testify to the great taste of these beans!—CB

Black-eyed Pea Salad

BEANS

1 tablespoon extra-virgin olive oil
1 medium onion, chopped
3 or 4 garlic cloves, minced
1 pound black-eyed peas, rinsed and drained
6 cups water
1 bay leaf
Salt to taste

DRESSING AND SALAD

¼ cup red wine vinegar or sherry vinegar
1 garlic clove, minced
Salt and pepper, freshly ground, to taste
1 to 2 teaspoons ground cumin, lightly toasted
1 teaspoon Dijon mustard
½ cup broth from the beans
⅓ cup extra-virgin olive oil
1 large red bell pepper, diced
½ cup chopped cilantro

Heat 1 tablespoon olive oil in a large, heavy soup pot over medium heat; add onion; and cook until tender, about 5 minutes. Add half the garlic. Once it is fragrant, about 30 seconds to 1 minute, add the black-eyed peas and the water. Simmer, skimming off any foam from the surface. Add the bay leaf and salt, to taste (1 to 2 teaspoons). Reduce the heat; cover; and simmer 30 minutes. Taste and adjust salt if needed. Add the remaining garlic; cover; and simmer until the beans are tender but intact. Remove from the heat; drain over a bowl. Transfer the beans to a large salad bowl.

In a small bowl, whisk together vinegar, garlic, salt, pepper, cumin, and mustard; add the bean broth and the olive oil; blend with the whisk. Taste and adjust seasonings. Toss dressing with the warm beans. Stir in the red pepper and cilantro. Serve warm or at room temperature. ❖

Cookout Potatoes

Nonstick cooking spray
1 medium onion, halved and thinly sliced
1½ pounds Yukon Gold potatoes, very thinly sliced
1⅓ cups shredded low-fat sharp cheddar cheese
⅓ cup real bacon bits
⅓ cup chopped bell pepper
½ teaspoon garlic salt

Spray a 9 × 9 × 2-inch foil pan liberally with nonstick cooking spray. Layer half the onions, potatoes, cheese, bacon bits, bell pepper, and garlic salt in pan; then layer the other half over the first. Cover the top tightly with foil, and grill over medium heat for 1 hour, rotating pan occasionally to avoid hot spots. ❖

CB's Grilled Potatoes with Bacon, Cheese & Roasted Jalapeños

2 large russet potatoes, scrubbed and dried
Olive oil
3 strips cooked center-cut bacon, crumbled
4 jalapeño peppers, roasted and diced
¼ cup shredded smoked Gouda cheese
¼ cup grated Parmesan cheese
¼ cup sour cream
2 tablespoons minced green onions
Coarse salt and black pepper, freshly ground
½ cup adobo sauce

The potatoes can be roasted a day in advance.

Preheat grill to high. Rub potatoes with the oil. Poke small holes in each end to allow steam to escape; then grill over high heat for about 1 hour, turning every 15 minutes. (Or roast on warming rack without turning.)

Slice cooked potatoes in half lengthwise. Scoop all but ¼ inch of the potato into a bowl. Leave the rest inside the skin.

Add the remaining ingredients to the bowl; mix; then spoon into the skins. Top with additional Gouda, and melt over indirect heat with the hood closed. Drizzle with the adobo sauce when serving. ❖

8 Servings • Prep: 10 min. • Bake: 1 hr.

Smoked Gouda Sweet Potatoes with Praline-Pecan Crumble

4 tablespoons butter, divided
2½ pounds sweet potatoes, peeled and cut into ¾-inch cubes
½ teaspoon salt
1 teaspoon Creole seasoning
8 ounces smoked Gouda, shredded
1½ cups cranberry juice
½ cup dark brown sugar
3 tablespoons flour
½ cup chopped pecans
⅛ teaspoon nutmeg

Preheat the oven to 375°F. Spread 1 tablespoon of butter over the bottom and sides of a 9 × 12-inch baking dish.

Layer the cubed sweet potatoes in the baking dish, and toss them with the salt, Creole seasoning, and smoked Gouda. Pour cranberry juice over the mixture. Cover the dish, and bake for 30 minutes.

In the meantime, melt the remaining butter in a saucepan over low heat. Stir in the brown sugar, flour, pecans, and nutmeg. Mix well, and set it aside until the potatoes and cheese finish baking.

Remove the casserole from the oven, and spoon the pecan mixture over top. Continue baking, uncovered, for an additional 30 minutes. ❖

Spicy Grilled Fries

1 tablespoon paprika
1 teaspoon freshly ground black pepper
1 teaspoon kosher salt
½ teaspoon chili powder
Pinch of cayenne (optional)
4 large russet or baking potatoes, scrubbed but not peeled
Olive oil

Preheat the grill to medium-low. Combine the first five ingredients in a small bowl. Cut the potatoes in half lengthwise; then slice each half into long wedges that are about ½ inch thick in the middle. Place the potatoes in a large plastic storage bag, and pour the oil on top. Shake well to coat; then sprinkle the potatoes generously with the spice mixture, and shake again until they are well coated. Place the potatoes directly on the grate, and grill for 30 to 35 minutes, turning every 5 to 7 minutes. Dab them lightly with additional oil as needed. The potatoes are ready when crisp and golden brown outside and soft in the middle. ❖

Grilled Potato Planks

1½ pounds (about 3 large) unpeeled baking potatoes, cut into ½-inch-thick slices
3 tablespoons olive oil
2 teaspoons finely chopped fresh rosemary
1 garlic clove, minced
½ teaspoon salt

Preheat grill to medium high. Combine oil, rosemary, garlic, and salt in dish. Add potato slices, and turn until well-coated. Grill potatoes for about 8 minutes. Turn, and continue grilling 10 minutes longer or until cooked. Remove from grill, and serve. ❖

Courtesy of www.christopherranch.com

Cranberry-Pecan Rice Pilaf

2 tablespoons butter or margarine
1 cup uncooked rice
1 can (14½ ounces) chicken broth
1 cup grated Parmesan cheese
½ cup dried cranberries
½ cup pecans, chopped and toasted*
¼ cup sliced green onions
Salt and black pepper, ground, to taste

**To toast pecans, spread nuts on small baking sheet. Bake 5 to 8 minutes at 350°F, or until golden brown, stirring frequently.*

Melt butter in 2-quart saucepan over medium heat. Add rice; cook, stirring, 2 to 3 minutes. Add broth, and heat to boiling, stirring once or twice. Reduce heat; cover; and simmer 15 minutes or until liquid is absorbed.

Remove from heat. Stir in cheese, cranberries, pecans, and onions. Season to taste with salt and pepper. ❖

Pan-Pacific Rice

1 cup long grain rice
1 cup sliced green onions
¾ cup salted cashews
¼ cup seasoned rice vinegar
1 tablespoon sesame seeds, toasted*

Prepare rice according to package directions; this should yield about 3 cooked cups. While rice is still hot, combine it with the onions, cashews, vinegar, and sesame seeds. Toss well. ❖

*To toast sesame seeds, spread them on a small baking sheet. Bake at 350°F for 5 to 8 minutes, stirring occasionally, or until golden brown.

Grilled Polenta

3 cups water
1 teaspoon salt
2 tablespoons unsalted butter
¾ cup polenta or coarse-ground yellow cornmeal
¾ cup freshly grated Parmesan cheese
¼ teaspoons cayenne pepper
Olive oil

Combine the water, salt, and butter in a saucepan, and bring to a boil. Gradually add the polenta, whisking constantly to avoid lumps. Reduce heat, and continue cooking, stirring constantly, until mixture is very thick, 10 to 15 minutes. Remove the pan from the heat, and stir in Parmesan cheese and cayenne pepper.

Line a 9-inch pie plate with plastic wrap, letting it extend over the edges. Spread the polenta evenly over plastic wrap, and smooth the top. Cover tightly with plastic wrap, and chill until firm, at least 1 hour.

Preheat the grill to medium. Invert the pie plate to allow molded polenta to be removed. Peel off the plastic wrap. Cut the polenta into six wedges. Brush each wedge lightly on both sides with oil. Arrange the polenta wedges on the cooking grate. Grill, turning 2 or 3 times, until golden, about 10 minutes. ❖

8–10 Servings • Prep: 10 min. • Grill: 30–35 min.

CB's Smoky, Cheesy Cornbread

1½ cups cornmeal
1 cup all-purpose flour
1 teaspooon baking soda
½ teaspooon salt
3 tablespoons sugar
¼ cup vegetable oil
2 large eggs
1 cup buttermilk
4 ounces smoked cheese, such as smoked Gouda or smoked blue cheese

Preheat grill to medium. Lightly grease a small cast-iron skillet or a 9 x 5 baking pan.

Whisk together first five ingredients; then add oil, eggs, and buttermilk; use spatula to mix until just combined. Ladle batter evenly into pan. Crumble cheese on top, and let rest for 15 minutes; then bake in grill over indirect heat for 30 to 35 minutes. (Check doneness by inserting a toothpick in the center; it should come out clean.) Remove, and cool for a few minutes. Run a butter knife around the edge; place cooling rack on top of skillet or pan; and flip. Cool for 30 minutes before slicing. ❖

Miss Allison's One-Beer Skillet Bread

3 cups self-rising flour
¼ cup sugar
Pinch salt
1 can beer
1 egg, beaten

OPTIONAL ADDITIONS

Sliced onions, corn, bacon bits, bell pepper, jalapeño, or chopped herbs

Preheat grill to medium low. Mix flour, sugar, salt, and beer, and lightly knead into a dough. Pour dough into a well-seasoned cast-iron skillet, or add a bit of bacon grease to the bottom and sides of a pan. Brush the top of the dough with the beaten egg; then top with the onions, corn, or other additions.

Place skillet on grill over indirect heat. Close lid. After about 50 minutes, move the skillet over direct heat, and continue cooking for 10 minutes.

Skillet bread is done when toothpick inserted in the center comes out clean. Flip bread over onto a cooling rack. Serve in wedges. ◆

8 Servings • Prep: 20 min. • Bake: 20 min.

Better-than-Mom's Mac & Cheese

1 box (16 ounces) corkscrew or mini penne pasta
¼ cup butter or margarine
¼ cup all-purpose flour
4 cups milk
¾ teaspoon salt
1½ teaspoons Tabasco sauce
1 cup shredded Gruyère cheese
1 cup shredded sharp cheddar cheese

BREAD-CRUMB TOPPING

⅓ cup butter or margarine
½ cup dried seasoned bread crumbs
½ teaspoon Tabasco sauce

Prepare pasta as directed on box. Drain; set aside.

Meanwhile, melt butter in 3-quart saucepan over medium heat. Stir in flour until blended and smooth. Gradually whisk in milk, salt, and Tabasco sauce. Cook until thickened and smooth, stirring often. Add cheese to sauce, and stir until melted. In large bowl, toss sauce with cooked pasta. Spoon mixture into an ungreased 2-quart baking dish.

Preheat oven to 375°F. To prepare bread-crumb topping, melt butter or magarine in a small skillet over medium heat. Stir in bread crumbs and Tabasco sauce; blend well. Top pasta mixture with prepared bread crumbs and cheese. Bake 20 minutes until crumbs are toasted and casserole is completely heated. ❖

Outstanding Onion Rings

1 giant-size sweet onion
1½ cups flour
1 teaspoon salt
¼ teaspoon freshly ground black pepper
⅛ teaspoon cayenne pepper
1½ cups buttermilk
Vegetable oil for frying
Popcorn salt, to taste

Peel the onion, removing the tough outer layer of the onion with the skin. Cut into horizontal slices about ½ inch thick. Separate the slices into individual rings.

Combine the flour, salt, black pepper, and cayenne in a shallow bowl; stir to mix. Pour the buttermilk into a separate bowl. Coat the onion rings, a few at a time, in the flour mixture, shaking off the excess, and place them in a baking dish. One or two at a time, dip the onion rings into buttermilk. Remove, and coat them again in the flour mixture, shaking off any excess. Transfer the rings back to the baking dish. Repeat the process with all the remaining onion rings.

Pour the oil to a depth of ½ to 1 inch in a cast-iron skillet or deep fryer, and heat over medium-high heat. When the temperature reaches 375°F, add onion rings a few at a time. Allow enough room for each of the onion rings to fry without touching one another. Cook, turning once, until deep golden brown on both sides, about 3 minutes. Remove the onion rings from the oil, and drain. While the onion rings are hot, salt them to taste. Be sure the oil returns to 375°F before frying additional rings. Serve at once, or place the onion rings on an ovenproof dish, and keep them warm in a 200°F oven until ready to serve. ❖

Uncle Jim's Time-Tested Grilled Corn

4 ears corn, still in husk
Olive oil for brushing
Garlic or onion, chopped and caramelized
Fresh herbs
Nutmeg
Sea salt
Black pepper

Pull back on each corn husk, but do not remove it. Remove and discard corn silk; then soak the cobs in a pot of cold water for 15 minutes. Preheat the grill to medium. Remove the corn from the water, and brush the kernels with olive oil. Spread corn with the caramelized garlic or onion, fresh herbs, nutmeg, sea salt, and black pepper. Tie the husks back in place with twine. Place the prepared ears of corn over direct heat on the grill, turning every few minutes to create grill marks. Finish the corn with indirect heat on the top shelf of the grill with the cover closed. Allow the corn to roast for another 15 minutes. ❖

Indian Spice-Grilled Cauliflower

4 tablespoons butter
¼ teaspoon cinnamon
¼ teaspoon dried coriander
½ teaspoon grated fresh ginger
⅛ teaspoon crushed saffron threads (optional)
¼ teaspoon ground cardamom
1 tablespoon minced garlic
1 head cauliflower, cut into florets

In a skillet, cook the butter over medium heat until golden brown. Combine the cinnamon, coriander, ginger, saffron, cardamom, and garlic; stir this mixture into the butter. Add the cauliflower, stirring to coat the florets with sauce, and cook for 3 to 4 minutes, stirring occasionally. Transfer the cauliflower florets to a grill basket, saving any remaining sauce for basting. Grill the vegetables over high heat, basting and turning them frequently. Cook for 5 minutes or until they are crunchy-tender. Be careful not to overcook. Serve. ◆

Creamy Zucchini & Garlic

2½ tablespoons butter
6 garlic cloves, minced
6 medium zucchini, grated
2½ tablespoons garlic powder
1 teaspoon chopped thyme
2½ tablespoons sour cream
Fresh pepper

Melt the butter in a heavy-bottom skillet over medium heat. Lower the heat; add the minced garlic; and sauté for about 1 to 2 minutes. (Do not let the garlic burn.) Add the grated zucchini, garlic powder, and thyme.

Cook, stirring frequently until the zucchini is tender. Remove from the heat, and stir in the sour cream. Season with fresh pepper. Serve immediately. ❖

Courtesy of www.christopherranch.com

Grilled Ratatouille

½ large red onion, quartered
1 package cherry tomatoes
2 zucchini, sliced
1 package sliced mushrooms
2 large yellow squash, sliced
1 red pepper, julienned
1 yellow pepper, julienned
1 green pepper, julienned
¾ cup balsamic vinegar
¼ cup Worcestershire sauce
1 tablespoon olive oil
1 tablespoon Creole seasoning
1 teaspoon seasoned salt

Combine ingredients in a large bowl; then in a plastic storage bag. Marinate in the refrigerator for at least 2 hours. Preheat grill to medium-high. Grill the mixture in a grill wok or a basket until the vegetables are tender, stirring occasionally. The vegetables are best when somewhat charred. ❖

8 Servings • Marinate: 30 min. • Prep: 15 min.

Asian Super Slaw

- 6 tablespoons rice vinegar
- 6 tablespoons vegetable oil
- 5 tablespoons creamy peanut butter
- 3 tablespoons soy sauce
- 3 tablespoons golden brown sugar, packed
- 2 tablespoons minced fresh ginger
- 1½ tablespoons minced garlic
- 5 cups thinly sliced green cabbage
- 2 cups thinly sliced red cabbage
- 2 large red or yellow bell peppers, cut into matchstick-size strips
- 2 medium carrots, peeled and cut into matchstick-size strips
- 8 large scallions, cut into matchstick-size strips
- ½ cup chopped fresh cilantro

This colorful, Asian-inspired salad is great with pork.

Whisk together the first seven ingredients in a small bowl until blended. Cover, and let chill. (The dressing can be made 1 day ahead.) Let the dressing stand at room temperature for 30 minutes before continuing.

Combine the remaining ingredients in a large bowl. Add the dressing, and toss to coat. Season the salad with salt and pepper, and serve. ❖

Pineapple Salsa

3 medium tomatoes, diced
1 large onion, finely chopped
¼ fresh pineapple, cut into chunks
1 clove garlic, minced
1 bunch of cilantro, chopped
Salt and pepper
Olive oil
Chili flakes

Combine tomatoes, onion, pineapple chunks, garlic, and cilantro in a medium bowl. Season with salt, pepper, olive oil, and chili flakes to taste. ❖

You Won't Know It's Not Potato Salad

2 1-pound bags frozen cauliflower florets
1 10-ounce bag frozen peas and carrots
1¾ cups reduced-fat mayonnaise or salad dressing
1 teaspoon granulated sugar
1 teaspoon salt
¼ teaspoon pepper
¼ teaspoon paprika
1 tablespoon cider vinegar
1 teaspoon yellow mustard
1 cup chopped celery (2½ stalks)
⅔ cup chopped onion (about 1 medium)
4 hard-boiled eggs, peeled, chopped, and cooled

Place cauliflower, peas, and carrots in a large microwavable bowl; cover with microwavable waxed paper. Cook on high 8 to 10 minutes or until tender, pausing halfway to stir; then continue to cook. Drain in colander, and rinse with cold water to stop cooking process. Place colander with vegetables over same bowl; refrigerate at least 30 minutes.

In a small bowl, make the dressing by combining the next seven ingredients; set aside.

Remove vegetables from refrigerator, and pat dry with paper towels; discard any liquid in bowl. Chop large florets into ¾-inch chunks. Return to bowl with the other vegetables, and add the celery, onion, and chopped eggs.

Coat with the dressing. If desired, cover and refrigerate at least 1 hour or until well-chilled before serving. ❖

Grilled Bruschetta

¼ cup butter, melted
1 tablespoon garlic, chopped
½ loaf day-old French bread, cut into 1-inch slices
5 tomatoes, seeded and cut into chunks
½ red onion, finely chopped
¼ cup extra-virgin olive oil
¼ cup balsamic vinegar
Salt and pepper to taste
1 tablespoon Italian parsley, coarsely chopped
1 tablespoon fresh basil leaves, coarsely chopped

Preheat the grill to medium-high. Melt the butter in a small saucepan; then add the chopped garlic. Brush the garlic butter on both sides of the bread slices. Grill the bread over medium-high heat until lightly browned, 3 to 4 minutes for each side.

Cut the grilled bread slices into quarters, and place them on a plate. Top with the chopped tomato and red onion. Drizzle the olive oil and balsamic vinegar over the top. Sprinkle with salt, pepper, parsley, and basil. Let stand about 30 minutes to allow the bread slices to absorb liquids. Serve at room temperature. ❖

145
150
151
153

5 Desserts

24 Servings • Prep: 20 min. • Grill: 16–18 min.

Bacon Chocolate-Chip Cookies

1 cup all-purpose flour
1 cup bread flour
½ teaspoon salt
½ teaspoon baking soda
1½ cup turbinado sugar or light brown sugar
¾ cup unsalted butter, melted
1 egg
1 egg yolk
⅛ teaspoon cinnamon
1 tablespoon vanilla extract
2 cups semisweet chocolate chips or chunks
¼ pound bacon, fried crisp and crumbled

Preheat the grill to 325°F, and set it up for indirect cooking. Grease cookie sheets, or line them with parchment paper or baking mats. Sift the flour, salt, and baking soda; set aside.

Using a mixer, combine the sugar and butter; add eggs, cinnamon, and vanilla; and mix until creamy. Blend in the sifted ingredients; then fold in the chocolate chips and crumbled bacon, using a spatula or a wooden spoon.

Drop ¼-cup-size dough balls onto a cookie sheet, spaced about 3 inches apart, and bake for 9 minutes; then turn and bake for an additional 7 to 9 minutes. Let the cookies cool slightly on the sheet for a few minutes before moving them to a rack to finish cooling.

Peanut Butter & Marshmallow Finger Sandwiches

½ cup heavy cream
2 ounces semisweet chocolate, chopped
1 pound cake
½ cup peanut butter
⅓ cup marshmallow creme
2 tablespoons unsalted butter, melted

In a microwave-safe bowl, heat cream and chocolate on high for 30 seconds; stir; heat for about another 30 seconds, making sure that cream does not boil. Let the mixture stand until the chocolate is melted, about 5 minutes, stirring occasionally.

Preheat the grill to medium high. Using a knife, trim off the top of the cake so that it is even on all sides. Cut the cake in half horizontally. Spread the peanut butter on one half and the marshmallow on the other. Put the two halves together, and brush the top and bottom with butter.

Grill, turning once, until both sides are warm and golden, about 3 to 5 minutes. Transfer to a platter, and cut the cake into thin finger sandwiches. Serve with the chocolate dipping sauce.

9 Servings • Prep: 15 min. • Grill: 30 min.

Grilled Brownie Sundae with Blueberry Sauce

BLUEBERRY SAUCE

¼ cup sugar
2 tablespoons lemon juice
2 cups blueberries, fresh or frozen

SUNDAE & TOPPINGS

Vanilla ice cream or frozen yogurt
Whipped cream (optional)
Chopped nuts (optional)

BROWNIES

½ cup sugar
2 tablespoons butter
2 tablespoons water
1½ cups semisweet chocolate chips
2 eggs, slightly beaten
½ teaspoon vanilla
⅔ cup flour
¼ teaspoon baking soda
½ teaspoon salt

In a small saucepan, bring the blueberry sauce ingredients to a boil. Stir for 1 minute, and remove from heat. Set aside. Bring sugar, butter, and water to a boil in a medium saucepan over low heat; remove from heat, and add chocolate chips, stirring until melted. Blend in eggs and vanilla. In a separate bowl, combine flour, baking soda, and salt; then add to the chocolate mixture.

Preheat grill to medium. Spoon batter into an oiled 9 × 9-inch metal pan. Bake over indirect heat with the lid down for 30 minutes or until a toothpick inserted into the center of the brownies comes out clean. Cool before slicing.

Scoop ice cream onto each brownie; sprinkle with nuts if desired; and drizzle sauce over the top.

Grilled S'mores

8 graham crackers, each one split in half to make 16 pieces
8 chocolate squares
16 large marshmallows
Skewers

Preheat the grill to high. If using wooden skewers, soak them in water before using them on the grill. Place the graham cracker halves on a warming tray. Set a square of chocolate on top of half of the crackers. Thread the marshmallows onto the end of each skewer. Hold the marshmallows just above the grill grate directly over high heat, turning slowly until lightly browned, about 2 to 3 minutes. Meanwhile, warm the graham crackers and chocolate over indirect heat. Place two roasted marshmallows on top of the melted chocolate, and gently press down with the top half of graham cracker. Serve immediately.

Grilled Banana Splits

2 tablespoons butter, melted
6 large ripe bananas
18 large scoops of your favorite ice cream
Chocolate sauce, as desired
Whipped cream, as desired
Chopped toasted nuts, as desired
6 maraschino cherries

Preheat the grill to medium. Melt the butter in a saucepan. Slice the bananas, still in their peels, lengthwise. Place the bananas cut side down onto the grates; grill for 3 to 4 minutes. Flip the bananas to the other side (peel side down). Brush the cut surfaces with melted butter, and grill for 2 to 3 additional minutes until the bananas are soft and light brown.

Remove the bananas from the grill, and let them cool. Remove the bananas from peels, and cut them into 1-inch chunks. Divide the cut bananas evenly among six serving dishes, and top each with three scoops of ice cream. Top each with chocolate sauce, whipped cream, nuts, and a cherry.

TIP: let your guests customize their own banana splits. Set up a banana-split bar with a variety of sauces and toppings.

Frozen Strawberry Pie

CRUST

4 tablespoons sugar
14 chocolate graham crackers, crushed
1 tablespoon butter, melted

FILLING

12 ounces white-chocolate chips
6 egg whites
1 pint heavy cream, sweetened
1 teaspoon vanilla
1 pound fresh strawberries
1 cup strawberry glaze or jelly

Combine sugar with chocolate graham crackers; add butter; press into a springform pan; and bake at 375°F for 6 to 7 minutes. Set aside to cool.

Melt white-chocolate chips in a double boiler, and let cool slightly. Beat egg whites until stiff, and then set aside. Whip the heavy cream with vanilla; set aside.

Wash the strawberries; pat dry with paper towels; and chop, reserving a few for garnish. Place into a bowl with the strawberry jelly. Fold the egg whites into the whipped cream; then fold in the strawberry mixture, followed by the white chocolate. Pour the filling into the pie crust, and freeze.

Remove the pie from the freezer about 15 minutes before serving to soften slightly. Garnish with the reserved strawberries.

8 Servings • Prep: 20 min. • Grill: 40–45 min.

Wood-Fired Apple-Pecan Pie

CRUST

1½ cups flour
¾ teaspoon salt
1½ tablespoons sugar
½ cup shortening
½ tablespoon butter
5 tablespoons water

FILLING

4 Granny Smith apples
3 Gala apples
2 cups pecans
1 cup brown sugar
1 tablespoon cinnamon
¾ cup flour

CRUMB TOPPING

1 cup flour
1 cup sugar
3 teaspoons cinnamon
½ cup (1 stick) butter, softened

For the crust, mix the flour, salt, and sugar. Cut in the shortening and butter. Mix in the water 1 tablespoon at a time using a fork. Roll out the dough, and shape it into a pie plate. Set aside.

For the filling, peel, core, and slice the apples; then mix them with the other filling ingredients. Place the mixture in the crust, creating a mound in the middle.

For the crumb top, mix the flour, sugar, and cinnamon in a bowl. Cut in the butter until the mixture forms pea-size crumbs. Cover the apples with the crumb topping. Bake the pie in a smoker at 375°F for 40 to 45 minutes or until golden brown.

Grilled Pineapple with Rum & Coconut

1 ripe pineapple, peeled and cut crosswise into 6 slices
2 to 3 tablespoons dark rum
1 teaspoon granulated sugar
1 cup whipped cream
¼ cup shredded coconut, toasted

With or without a scoop of ice cream, this grilled dessert will be a huge hit at your next outdoor party.

Pour the rum and sugar in a bowl with the pineapple. Mix to coat the slices evenly; cover with plastic wrap; and let it rest for 3 to 5 minutes. Preheat the grill to medium high.

Lightly sear the pineapple directly over the heat for about 10 minutes, using tongs to turn once. Make sure the fruit does not become overly charred.

Remove pineapple from grill, and top with whipped cream and coconut. You can also add a heaping scoop of your favorite ice cream if desired.

CB's Nutella & Marshmallow Quesadillas

4 soft flour tortillas
8 tablespoons Nutella or thick chocolate sauce
8 tablespoons marshmallow creme
2 tablespoons butter, melted (½ tablespoon per tortilla)
2 teaspoons cinnamon
2 teaspoons sugar

Preheat grill to low. Warm, but do not brown, the tortillas; then lay them flat on a work surface. Spread 2 tablespoons of Nutella and 2 tablespoons of marshmallow creme on top of each one; fold them in half; and return them to the grill. Cover with an inverted aluminum pan for quick heating.

When the Nutella and marshmallow are sufficiently heated and oozing slightly out of the tortillas, remove the quesadillas from the grill, and quickly brush them with melted butter. Finish with a sprinkling of cinnamon and sugar. Serve warm.

CB's Grilled Pears with Honey & Thyme

Canola oil spray
1 ripe pear, cored and sliced into eighths
1 tablespoon honey
1 teaspoon chopped fresh thyme

This easy dessert will cook quickly, especially if the grill is already hot.

Preheat the grill to medium. Spray the pear slices with canola oil, and grill, turning as needed, until they are slightly soft and grill marks appear. Arrange four slices in a fan shape on each plate. Drizzle with honey, and sprinkle with thyme. Serve as is or with a dollop of ice cream or whipped cream if desired.

Mississippi River Pie

- **1½ cups crumbled chocolate sandwich cookies**
- **2 tablespoons unsalted butter, melted**
- **1½ quarts coffee ice cream**
- **1 cup chunky-style peanut butter**
- **8 ounces semisweet chocolate chips**
- **2 cups heavy cream**
- **1½ tablespoons confectioners' sugar**

Preheat the oven to 350°F. Combine the crumbled cookies together with the melted butter in a medium bowl. Press the crumb mixture over the bottom of a 10-inch springform pan. Bake for about 14 to 16 minutes or until firm. Chill the crust in the freezer for about 15 minutes.

Place the ice cream in a large bowl, and allow it to soften slightly. Stir in the peanut butter; then press the mixture into the chilled crust. Quickly return the ice cream to the freezer for about 2 hours.

Just before serving, remove ice cream from the freezer. Next, make the chocolate sauce by slowly melting the chocolate chips and ½ cup of cream in a microwave or over a double boiler. Whip the remaining 1½ cups of cream until soft peaks form. Sprinkle the cream with sugar, and continue whipping until stiff peaks form. Release the pie from the springform pan, and cut it into wedges. To serve, pour warm chocolate sauce over each wedge, and top with whipped cream.

Rice Pudding with Dark-Chocolate Sauce

5 ounces uncooked white rice
2 pints milk
7 tablespoons butter
½ teaspoon vanilla extract
⅓ cup sugar
¼ teaspoon nutmeg

FOR THE SAUCE:

5 ounces dark-chocolate chips
2 tablespoons water
1 tablespoon butter

In a medium saucepan, combine the rice, milk, butter, vanilla, nutmeg, and sugar. Bring the mixture to a gentle simmer over medium-high heat. Reduce the heat to low; cover; and simmer until the mixture is thick and pudding-like, about 10 minutes. Be careful not to scorch the bottom.

In a separate saucepan, heat the chocolate, water, and butter over low heat, and stir until the mixture is smooth and shiny, about 5 minutes. Add 2 to 3 heaping spoonfuls of chocolate sauce to each serving of the rice pudding.

This dessert is courtesy of Adam Byrd, who says, "This is the most decadent thing I have made to date."

160
161
164
166

6 Marinades, Sauces & Rubs

Plum Marinade

Yield: approx. ¾ cup
Prep: 5 min.
Marinate: 4–6 hr.
Use with: steak

½ cup plum preserves
3 tablespoons minced green onion
2 tablespoons white vinegar
2 tablespoons hoisin sauce
2 teaspoons minced fresh ginger
1 teaspoon dry mustard
½ teaspoon ground red pepper
Green onion, minced (optional)

In a bowl, whisk together all of the ingredients until completely emulsified. Marinate meat in a sealable plastic bag or covered container in the refrigerator.

Three-Way Marinade

Yield: 1 cup
Prep: 5 min.
Marinate: 4–12 hr.
Use with: flank steak, London broil

CLASSIC MARINADE

1 cup prepared Italian-style vinaigrette
1 teaspoon minced garlic
¼ teaspoon coarsely ground black pepper

MEXICAN VARIATION

To classic marinade, add
1 tablespoon fresh lime juice
1 teaspoon ground cumin
1 teaspoon chipotle chili powder
½ teaspoon salt

ASIAN VARIATION

To classic marinade, add
2 tablespoons reduced-sodium soy sauce
2 tablespoons minced fresh ginger
1 tablespoon packed brown sugar
1 tablespoon sesame seeds, toasted
1½ teaspoons dark sesame oil

In a bowl, whisk together all ingredients until completely emulsified. Marinate meat in a sealable plastic bag or covered container in the refrigerator.

Captain Jessie's Jamaican Jerk Marinade

Yield: 1 cup
Prep: 10 min.
Marinate: 4 hr.–overnight
Use with: beef and pork

1 white onion, chopped
½ cup chopped scallions
2 teaspoons fresh thyme or
1 teaspoon dried thyme

Spices from the Caribbean give this marinade a kick to heat up your mouth!

1 whole Scotch Bonnet or habanero pepper, seeded and chopped
1 teaspoon coarse salt
2 teaspoons light brown sugar
1 teaspoon allspice
½ teaspoon ground nutmeg
½ teaspoon ground cinnamon
1 teaspoon black pepper
1 tablespoon soy sauce
1 tablespoon Worcestershire sauce
1 tablespoon vegetable oil
1 tablespoon apple cider vinegar

In a food processor or blender, add the onions, scallions, thyme, and peppers. Stir in the other ingredients, and pulse until mixture becomes a light slurry. Marinate meat in a sealable plastic bag or covered container in the refrigerator.

NOTE: when working with fresh peppers, use food-safe gloves; do not touch your eyes, mouth, or nose until you have washed your hands with soap and water.

Korean Kalbi Marinade

Yield: approx. 1 cup
Prep: 5 min.
Marinate: overnight
Use with: short ribs

1 tablespoon soy sauce
¼ cup sugar
2 tablespoons honey
¼ cup Chinese rice wine
2 teaspoons Korean toasted-sesame oil
2 green onions, minced
4 teaspoons (1 to 2 cloves) chopped garlic
2 tablespoons toasted sesame seeds
2 tablespoons water
1 teaspoon grated ginger root

The recipe is a classic one used for most Korean kalbi (grilled short ribs).

Mix ingredients in a nonreactive bowl. Use some as an overnight marinade for meat—placed in a sealable plastic bag or covered container in the refrigerator—and reserve some for glazing during the final 5 to 7 minutes of cooking.

Avocado Cream

Yield: 1½ cups
Prep: 30 min.
Use with: Garlic-Lime Alaska Prawns (See page 69.)

2 avocados, 1½ pounds total
½ cup sour cream
2 tablespoons mayonnaise
2 tablespoons lime juice
1 teaspoon ground dried ancho chiles or chili powder
½ teaspoon salt

Peel ripe avocados; cut into chunks; and put in the work bowl of a food processor. Add sour cream, mayonnaise, lime juice, ancho chiles or chili powder, and salt; blend until smooth. Taste, and add more lime juice and salt if desired. Scrape into small bowl.

Maître d' Butter

Yield: 2 cups
Prep: 10 min.
Refrigerate: 1 hr. or overnight
Use with: steak, fish, vegetables

1 pound (4 sticks) unsalted butter, softened
3 tablespoons lemon juice (about 1 lemon)
¼ cup chopped Italian (flat-leaf) parsley, or other herbs or spices as desired

In a large bowl, mash the butter. Add lemon juice and parsley and, using a wooden spoon, blend.

Spread a 1-foot-square piece of plastic wrap across a work surface, and scoop the butter mixture on top. Gently wrap the plastic film around the butter, forming a cylinder. Tie off the ends of the wrap with string or a twist tie. Chill or freeze until needed.

Maître d' Butter is simply softened butter with seasonings that is rolled and chilled. You can serve it in slices on top of grilled steaks, fish, or vegetables. Experiment by combining your favorite herbs and spices.

Spicy Grilled-Veggie Marinade

Yield: 1½ cups
Prep: 5 min.
Marinate: 1 hr.
Use with: vegetables

⅔ cup white wine vinegar
½ cup soy sauce
2 tablespoons minced fresh ginger
2 tablespoons olive oil
2 tablespoons sesame oil
2 large cloves garlic, minced
2 teaspoons Tabasco sauce

In a bowl, whisk together all ingredients until completely emulsified. Marinate in a sealable plastic bag or covered container in the refrigerator.

CB's Wet Salt Rub for Fish

Prep: 5 min.
Use with: fish

1 part coarse salt
1 part finely minced fresh lemon thyme
½ part anchovy paste
2½ parts dry white vermouth

Whisk together all ingredients until blended.

Savannah Smoker's Mohunken Rub

Yield: 3+ cups
Prep: 5 min.
Use with: pork

½ cup brown sugar
1 cup white sugar
1 cup paprika
¼ cup garlic powder
¼ cup coarse salt
2 tablespoons chili powder
2 teaspoons cayenne pepper
4 teaspoons black pepper
2 teaspoons dried oregano or Italian seasoning
2 teaspoons cumin
1 tablespoon mustard power
Yellow mustard to taste

Blend all ingredients in a small bowl.

Provençal Citrus-Tarragon Sauce

Yield: 1½ cups
Prep: 5 min.
Use with: halibut, salmon crab, scallops

¼ cup apple cider vinegar
2 tablespoons Dijon mustard
⅓ cup olive oil
2 tablespoons honey
⅓ cup fresh tarragon leaves
1 can (11 ounces) mandarin orange slices, drained, or 2 fresh mandarin oranges, peeled, sectioned, and seeded
½ teaspoon coarse salt

Combine the vinegar and mustard in a blender or food processor, and pulse until smooth; slowly add olive oil until fully incorporated. Add the honey, tarragon, and oranges; blend or pulse again until almost smooth. Salt to taste.

Green-Chili Pesto

Yield: approx. 2 cups
Prep: 15 min.
Use with: meat and fish

6 large, long green chilies or 4 medium poblano chilies, roasted, peeled, and seeded
¾ cup pine nuts
2 cups lightly packed fresh basil leaves and stems
6 garlic cloves, chopped
1 cup extra-virgin olive oil
¾ cup grated Parmesan cheese
½ cup grated Romano cheese
½ teaspoon salt
½ teaspoon ground black pepper

Chop the chilies, and set aside.

In a skillet over medium heat, toast the pine nuts; then let them cool to room temperature.

In a food processor, combine chilies, pine nuts, basil, and garlic. Process, scraping down sides of the bowl once or twice, until smooth. Drizzle in olive oil. Transfer the mixture to a bowl, and blend in the cheese, salt, and pepper. Use immediately, or cover and refrigerate for up to 3 days; freeze (without cheese) for up to 3 months.

Moroccan Sauce

Discover the flavors of North Africa in this zesty sauce made using fiery-hot harissa, a traditional seasoning for couscous. If harissa is not available, substitute 1 tablespoon of pimenton (smoked Spanish paprika).

Yield: approx. 1 cup
Prep: 5 min.
Cook: 12–13 min.
Use with: cod, halibut, salmon, crab, scallops

1½ tablespoons minced garlic
½ cup olive oil
½ cup unsalted butter
2 tablespoons harissa
1½ tablespoons fresh lemon juice or 1 to 2 tablespoons sherry
Coarse salt, to taste
Cracked black pepper, to taste
2 tablespoons chopped Italian (flat-leaf) parsley
2 tablespoons chopped salted almonds (optional)

Place the garlic, olive oil, and butter in a small saucepan over low heat. Cook until the garlic begins to soften, about 10 minutes. Add the harissa and lemon juice, blending with a whisk; continue cooking 2 to 3 minutes more. Season to taste with salt and pepper. Garnish with parsley and, if desired, almonds.

Adobo Marinade

Yield: 1 cup
Prep: 5–10 min.
Marinate: 2 hr.–overnight
Use with: pork or fish

½ cup fresh orange juice
2 tablespoons lime juice
2 tablespoons wine vinegar
3 canned chipotle chilis
3 garlic cloves
2 teaspoons oregano
½ teaspoon black pepper
½ teaspoon salt
½ teaspoon ground cumin

In the bowl of a food processor, place all ingredients; puree. Makes enough marinade for six to eight pork chops. Place meat in self-sealing plastic bag; add marinade.

Adobo means seasoning or marinade in Spanish. This dark-red marinade is often used in Filipino and Puerto Rican cooking.—CB

Chipotle Marinade

Yield: ½ cup
Prep: 5–10 min.
Marinate: 2 hr.–overnight
Use with: steak or seafood

⅓ cup fresh lime juice
¼ cup chopped fresh cilantro
1 tablespoon packed brown sugar
2 teaspoons minced chipotle chilies in adobo sauce
2 tablespoons adobo sauce (from chilies)
2 cloves garlic, minced

Combine ingredients well; then pour marinade over meat or seafood. Marinate in a plastic ziplock bag or covered dish in the refrigerator.

This Southwestern marinade is great for flank steak or pork tenderloin.—CB

George JV's Secret Beef Jerky Marinade

Yield: 1 cup
Prep: 5–10 min.
Marinate: 6 hr.–overnight
Use with: beef ribs, brisket, steak

½ cup soy sauce
1 clove garlic, mashed
2 tablespoons brown sugar
2 tablespoons ketchup
½ cup Worcestershire sauce
1¼ teaspoons salt
½ teaspoon onion powder
½ teaspoon pepper

Marinate in plastic bag or covered container in the refrigerator for at least 6 hours or overnight.

George JV is a "Sizzle On the Grill" reader and frequent recipe contributor.—CB

Quick Chimichurri Marinade

Yield: 1½ cups
Prep: 5–10 min.
Marinate: 2 hr.–overnight
Use with: London broil, flank steak, filet mignon

¾ cup prepared, non-creamy Caesar dressing
½ cup chopped fresh parsley
¾ teaspoon crushed red pepper
Salt and pepper

Combine ingredients well; then pour marinade over meat. Marinate in a plastic ziplock bag or covered dish in the refrigerator.

Chimichurri originated in Argentina where it is a popular accompaniment to all types of grilled meats, especially steak.—CB

CB's Basic Beer Sauce

Yield: 3 cups
Prep: 15 min.
Use with: smoked beef brisket, pork butt, ribs

1 12-ounce can or bottle of ale or dark beer
½ cup apple cider
½ cup water
¼ cup peanut oil
2 medium shallots, chopped
3 garlic cloves, chopped
1 tablespoon Worcestershire sauce
1 teaspoon hot sauce

Combine the ingredients in a saucepan. Heat the mixture, and brush it on the meat during the final minutes of grilling.

Beer seems to be plentiful around many backyard barbecues. Try using a richer beer to make this excellent "mop" for your low- and slow-cooking barbecue or grilled meats.—CB

Memphis BBQ Sauce

Yield: 3 cups
Prep: 15 min.
Cook: 25 min.
Use with: pork ribs, beef ribs, brisket, pork butt

¼ cup apple cider vinegar
½ cup prepared mustard
2 cups ketchup
3 tablespoons Worcestershire sauce
1 tablespoon finely ground black pepper
¼ cup brown sugar
2 teaspoons celery salt
2 tablespoons chili powder
1 tablespoon onion powder
2 teaspoons garlic powder
¼ to ½ teaspoon cayenne pepper (optional)
2 teaspoons liquid smoke (optional)
2 tablespoons canola oil

Combine all ingredients, except the oil, in a saucepan. Bring them to a boil, stirring to dissolve the sugar. Reduce the heat, and simmer for 25 minutes, stirring occasionally. Using a whisk, blend in the oil until incorporated.

Horseradish Sauce

Yield: 1½ cups
Prep: 15 min.
Use with: smoked prime rib

1 3-ounce package cream cheese
1 cup sour cream
1 teaspoon grated onion
2 tablespoons horseradish
¼ teaspoon sugar
¼ teaspoon salt
¼ teaspoon pepper

Combine all ingredients in a blender.

This is a perfect accompaniment to a smoked rib roast.—CB

CB's Southwest-Style Rub

Yield: 1 cup
Prep: 10 min.
Marinate: 20 min.
Use with: pork, beef

DRY INGREDIENTS

¼ cup chili powder
¼ cup packed brown sugar
⅛ cup ground cumin
⅛ cup kosher salt
⅛ cup black pepper
1 teaspoon ground cinnamon

WET INGREDIENTS

1 tablespoon Worcestershire sauce
⅛ cup apple cider vinegar
1 tablespoon minced fresh garlic (or 1 tablespoon garlic powder)
1 teaspoon hot sauce

Mix the dry ingredients; add the wet ingredients; mix again. Store mixture in the refrigerator for up to 3 days. Apply the rub to meat; let meat rest for about 20 minutes before slow cooking. Note: use plastic gloves or plastic sandwich bags over your hands to prevent irritation from the spices.

I developed this rub to please guests who enjoy something a little spicy on their ribs or other slow-cooked meat. I think it works well with just about any meat, but particularly with pork when rubbed on about 20 minutes or so before you start the slow-cooking process."—CB

Resources

This list of manufacturers and associations is meant to be a general guide to additional industry and product-related sources. It is not intended as a listing of all of the products and manufacturers presented in this book.

Companies and Associations

THE ALASKA SEAFOOD MARKETING INSTITUTE (ASMI)
www.alaskaseafood.org
Alaska's official seafood marketing agency offers a consumer recipe database on its Web site.

CATTLEMEN'S BEEF BOARD AND NATIONAL CATTLEMEN'S BEEF ASSOCIATION
www.beefitswhatsfordinner.com
The beef industry offers tips, food safety information, and recipes for preparing beef through its Web site.

CHAR-BROIL
www.charbroil.com
This is the official Web site for the Char-Broil company.

CHRISTOPHER RANCH
www.christopherranch.com
Christopher Ranch provides product information and recipes on its Web site.

LOUISIANA SEAFOOD PROMOTION & MARKETING BOARD
http://louisianaseafood.com
The organization's Web site features news, information, and recipes.

NATIONAL PORK BOARD
www.porkbeinspired.com
The National Pork Board's-sponsored Web site features information, nutrition, and recipes.

SIZZLE ON THE GRILL
www.sizzleonthegrill.com
Char-Broil sponsors this newsletter and Web site, which features grilling tips and recipes.

MY BEEF CHECKOFF
www.beefboard.org
The Cattlemen's Beef Board-sponsored Web site provides consumer and industry information and recipes.

UNITED STATES DEPARTMENT OF AGRICULTURE (USDA) FOOD SAFETY AND INSPECTION SERVICE
www.fsis.usda.gov
The Web site offers consumer safety information on buying, storing, preparing, and cooking meat and poultry.

USDA MEAT & POULTRY HOTLINE
888-MPHotline
This hotline answers questions about safe storage, handling, and preparation of meat and poultry products.

Food Blogs and Recipe Databases

COOKTHINK
www.cookthink.com
This website features a recipe database and kitchen tips.

JESS THOMSON
www.jessthomson.wordpress.com
Jess Thomson is a Seattle-based, Bert Greene Award-nominated food writer, recipe developer, and food photographer.

"Sizzle on the Grill" Contributors

GIRLS ON A GRILL
www.girlsonagrill.com
These guest chefs are sisters who share their recipes featuring fresh ingredients cooked over an open fire.

GUIDE TO BASIC BEEF CUTS

TENDER STEAKS: most of these come from the center (rib and loin sections) and are best cooked using dry-heat methods such as grilling.

Premium tender steaks include top loin (strip), T-Bone, Porterhouse, ribeye, rib, and tenderloin.

Family-priced tender steaks include shoulder center, top sirloin, top blade (flat iron), chuck eye, and round tip.

LESS-TENDER STEAKS: these are primarily from the more muscled fore- and hind-quarters and are better suited for moist-heat cooking. However, some less-tender cuts may be cooked with dry heat after being tenderized. Less-tender steaks include round, top round, eye round, bottom round, chuck shoulder, chuck 7-bone, chuck arm, chuck blade, flank, and skirt.

CUBED STEAKS: these are mechanically tenderized steaks, usually from the round.

Courtesy of the Cattlemen's Beef Board and National Cattlemen's Beef Association

Index

D

E

F

G

T

U

V

W

Y

Z